Don't Never Be Afraid of Your Horses

This book would not have been possible
without the generosity of:

MR. & MRS. DUKE R. LIGON
DARRYL & KATHY SMETTE

ANN S. ALSPAUGH
THE CHICKASAW NATION
KEN & MARY ANN FERGESON
THE KERR FOUNDATION, INC.
STEVE & MILAH LYNN
JOHN & CHARLOTTE RICHELS
DICK SIAS

OKLAHOMA VOICES SERIES

Don't Never Be Afraid of Your Horses

LOOKING BACK
BY MIKE LARSEN

SERIES EDITOR: GINI MOORE CAMPBELL

OKLAHOMA HALL of FAME
PUBLISHING

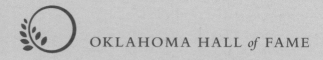

OKLAHOMA HALL *of* FAME

ISBN: 978-1-938923-34-0
Library of Congress Control Number: 2017936884

DESIGNED BY SKIP MCKINSTRY

Our first kiss as Mr. & Mrs.

A toast to the new couple

This book is dedicated to my wife Martha—
the love of my life.
I hunger for her when we are apart.

If she could only whistle . . . oh well.

Beautiful Dove by Mike Larsen. The image is of Larsen's daughter Kate. Beautiful Dove is her Indian name.

CONTENTS

FOREWORD

During high school, Mike Larsen made money on his first award-winning painting, a fan. He earned a whopping $15.

Mike Larsen is an Oklahoma treasure.

He is best known as a talented and celebrated artist whose works are included in museums and private collections around the world. Mike's style is distinctive, with a wide range of subject matter, but always with a story to be discovered in the composition, colors, and contrasts. Even more amazing is his ability to express his creativity in both two-dimensional paintings on canvas and three-dimensional sculptures in clay and bronze. Some are small and delicate; others are large and monumental. Mike's place in art history is already assured.

Just as important to me is Mike's talent as a historian. He may not have a Ph.D., but he has the instincts and skills of a historian who is always asking questions and seeking answers that can be expressed for the enjoyment of others. When Betty Price and the Oklahoma Arts Council chose Mike to paint a mural in the State Capitol commemorating our Five Indian Ballerinas, he not only captured the images of the dancers but placed them against a backdrop of their cultural roots that binds them together as a band of sisters.

Mike's skills as a historian served him well when Governor Bill Anoatubby asked him to paint portraits of Chickasaw elders. With the assistance of his life partner and wife, Martha, he interviewed the elders, studied their stories, and captured their images with a depth that comes only from a profound understanding of human nature, tribal history, and sense of community. The magic of combining artistic expression with historic insight can be seen in all of Mike's work.

Finally, Mike is known far and wide as a great friend. His gentle nature, generosity, and genuine interest in other people make him a welcome guest around the world and his stories always put a smile on the faces of his friends. Mike is one of those people who earn respect through the way they live their lives. When he asks for a favor, we friends feel privileged to be asked.

It was in the spirit of friendship that Mike and Martha asked me to read some of his written stories that were roughly autobiographical. Of course, I immediately agreed to read them as a friend. As I went through the stories, I quickly reverted back to my respect for Mike as an artist and historian. Each story, like his paintings, was composed with a careful blend of color and contrast. And each story had a depth of understanding, whether it was a peek into the nature of a character in his narrative or an insight into his own personality. I immediately urged him to write more, and just as importantly, to not change a word. Each story was written just as Mike would tell it in person.

I want to thank the Oklahoma Hall of Fame for bringing these stories to a wider audience. Mike will be remembered as a friend, historian, and artist. This book will expand his legacy to storyteller and author.

BOB L. BLACKBURN, PH.D.

Mike Larsen in his studio.

ACKNOWLEDGMENTS

As in any book, especially an autobiography, there are many people to thank.

I'd like to start with my family. Martha and I have been so blessed to put this family together and they are, after all, the most important people in the world.
  Kate Larsen and her two boys Logan and Nolan Hard
  Jeffrey and Erica Fransen
  Randall and Larissa Fransen

I'd like to thank my family of origin –
  My Mother Ruth Carter Larsen
  My Papa and Grandma – Otto and Lela Carter

I'd like to thank my family of friends -
  Leo, Dr. Bob Blackburn, Gov. Bill Anoatubby,
Betty Price, Ann Sherman, and Yvonne Chouteau.

I can't forget Jake and Old Son of a Bitch—maybe they should be first.

Without our family at the Oklahoma Hall of Fame, especially Gini Moore Campbell, this book would still be a dream.

And of course, our family of donors—the late Ann S. Alspaugh, The Chickasaw Nation, Ken and Mary Ann Fergeson, The Kerr Foundation, Inc., Steve and Milah Lynn, John and Charlotte Richels, and Dick Sias. Special thanks to Duke R. Ligon and Darryl and Kathy Smette who made the final substantial contributions to put us over the top.

Mike Larsen's 1956-1957 school-year picture while living in Wynnewood.

Martha Jane Schroeder in elementary school.

INTRODUCTION

In 1944 a baby named James Michael "Mike" was born to Ruth and Manly Lanham in Dallas, Texas. Manly did not stick around for the raising of "Little Mike" and his brother. In the early 1950's Ruth married Knude Larsen and Little Mike officially became Mike Larsen.

Mike's early childhood was split between living with his grandparents in Wynnewood, Oklahoma, and the Texas Elks Hospital in Luling, Texas, where he recovered from Polio and learned to walk again. By grade school his family was living in Amarillo, Texas. With the exception of a few years back in Wynnewood, where his mother owned a café named Ruth's, he spent the rest of his childhood in Amarillo.

Encouraged by a class in art his senior year at Tascosa High School in Amarillo, Mike decided to major in Art in college. He attended Amarillo Junior College, eventually transferring to the University of Houston where he quit one semester shy of earning his degree. After leaving the University of Houston, Mike painted and did odd jobs until he finally committed to art full time, some 45 years ago. Much to our children's later delight, his last "real" job was as a short order cook. He still makes the best hamburgers in the world.

This was the early 1970's and Mike discovered that by working in his studio during the week and traveling to art shows on the weekends, he could make a living. Later those art shows became major arts festivals and he succeeded beyond his wildest dreams. Mike had only one fan during this time that believed in him and considered art an occupation and a calling. That fan was his mother, Ruth. Mike married and had a daughter, Kate, who was the light of his life.

In 1953 I was born to Carl and Flonnie Schroeder in Hutchinson, Kansas. They named me Martha Jane. My father worked for Champlin Petroleum and was also a shop steward. My mother was a homemaker. My father was transferred to Enid, Oklahoma, where the family prospered and expanded. Four of the six Schroeder kids went to Oklahoma State University (this plays an important part later in the story).

Because my parents were hard working people, I learned that I could do pretty much anything I set my mind to. I took art classes, made most of my clothes, and went to OSU where I received my "Mrs. Degree." Married young, I started a picture framing business and had two sons.

By the late 1980's Mike and I both found ourselves divorced and started dating. In 1990 we married and started life with three children—ages 5, 6 and 9. It gets better. Within six months of marriage Mike was diagnosed with cancer and our studio over "The Jesus is Lord Pawn Shop" at Northwest 23rd and Villa in Oklahoma City, Oklahoma, burned. A month later our house nearly burned because two neighbor kids were playing with gasoline and matches on a very windy day. God

Mike with Randall, Kate, and Jeffrey.

spared all the neighborhood houses that day, but our pastor at the time told us we should start to take all of this personally.

The tide of bad news turned in April when Mike was given two pieces of good news within 10 minutes of each other— he won a commission to paint the Indian ballerina mural for the Oklahoma State Capitol and a painting of his had been selected for the June, 1991 cover of *Southwest Art* Magazine.

We were just getting started.

MARTHA LARSEN, 2017

EVERY DAY IS A PICNIC

Sketches—
OUR LIFE IN THE ARTS

If I were to be asked to explain my life in three words, I would simply say, "It's a sketch."

It seems that we are always working toward a finished product but, thankfully, we never get there. Over the span of my life, I have produced more sketches for paintings than I could possibly count. During the course of a painting, many sketches will be done, adjustments made, more sketches, and sketches directly on the painting with brush.

Sometimes I'll have to stop on the highway to put down an image or idea. A lot of time, these sketches are so vague I can't do anything with them. Sometimes though, they become something really exciting.

Martha is always sketching down things that I can't make hide nor tail of, but it doesn't matter because she knows.

I always have working sketches close by when I'm on the easel. I rely on them. Sometimes, the sketch will become the only work because it cannot be improved on.

I sometimes wish the things I see in my head could immediately be transferred to canvas, but that can't be. First, they must become a sketch. The closest I have come to that happening, was when I proposed to Martha. If I had tried to sketch that out, I would have surely screwed it up.

The events of our lives, like a good sketch, require planning, adjustment, and consideration. A smudge can change mood or a strong line can express power. A lot of negative space can create thought in the viewer, and hope.

This is a story of Martha's and my life in art, and we are still sketching.

Thank God.

Proud of his Chickasaw heritage, in *Mike and the Chickasaws* Mike Larsen included himself in the image.

The sketches behind and "work in progress" Mike Larsen is creating for the new offices of Heritage Trust in downtown Oklahoma City's historic *Journal Record* building.

The initial sketch dated May 28, 2014 and the completed work of art entitled *They Ruled the Plains*.

Don't Never Be
Afraid of Your Horses

Otto P. "Papa" Carter and his team of work horses. It is believed the horses were a Percheron mix. Percherons were believed to have been established in France during the Mediaeval Crusades. The title of the book, *Don't Never Be Afraid of Your Horses*, is a quote Larsen grew up hearing from his Papa.

Don't Never Be Afraid of Your Horses

1952

When I was little, my brother and I lived with my grandparents. I can still remember the way my granddad smelled, like Vitalis Hair Tonic for Men and Lucky Strike cigarettes. My Papa, Otto P. Carter, made a passable living for the time because he had a wagon and a team of very large horses. The names of the horses were Jake and Old Son of a Bitch. It wasn't until I was much older that I discovered the name of the second horse was actually Jim.

I would go out with Papa some mornings and watch him hitch up the team. He always harnessed Jake first, Jim second. I remember that Jim was a nervous animal and Papa would make me stand some distance away.

Papa was a small man, maybe 5′7″ or 5′8″ and wore a tall black hat with no crease. I found out later the reason he harnessed Jake first was because he was the "rock."

Toddler Mike Larsen when he lived with his grandparents in Wynnewood, Oklahoma.

Otto and Lela Carter, Mike Larsen's graandparents.

Once Papa had all the harness on both horses, Jim would still be nervous and hop and kick. Papa would walk up to the horse, look up into his eye, rear back, and punch Jim right in the throat. He would stand really close and yell, "All right you old son of a bitch, settle down." Jim would be good for the rest of the day.

One morning after this had happened, Papa climbed up on the wagon, looked down at me, and said, "Son, don't never be afraid of your horses."

Being self-employed is a risky business. Being an artist is a risky business. There are many obstacles to innovation and you have to learn early paths around those obstacles. You must never be afraid of a challenge. Never, ever be afraid of failure. Never be afraid of becoming great. Never be afraid of competition. I do my best work when I know that I have to do better work than someone else.

Don't never be afraid of your horses.

The risk is a measurement we all place on ourselves.

We have been fortunate over the years to become friends with some of the best artists in this country. These people didn't become great by accident. They became great because they were willing to risk failure and bad times while they were developing something really unique that they would continue to improve on for the rest of their lives.

Failure is a mighty big horse and I have a mighty good name for him.

Making Bread

Miss Isle Ford ran a boarding house and a lunchroom in Oklahoma City. Lunch, all you can eat, for twenty-five cents.

Miss Isle stood at the door as a young girl held up a sign that had been taped to the window. The sign read, "Help Wanted."

"I want to ask you about the job?" the girl inquired.

"Why honey," Miss Isle said, "you're just a child."

"I'm fourteen, I'm married, and I promise I'll work really hard," said the girl.

Miss Isle was a slight woman with grey hair set in very tight curls. She had on a pink dress with a flower print. The apron she wore fell nearly to the floor and her hose were rolled down to her ankles. She smelled lightly of bacon grease. Her eyes were intensely blue behind wire-rimmed glasses.

The Dance by Mike Larsen.

Miss Isle Ford operated the boarding house and lunchroom in Oklahoma City that Larsen's mother started worked for at the age of 14. It was there she learned to make bread—a tradition Larsen carries on today.

Mike Larsen's mother, Ruth.

"You work for me, girl, and I can guarantee you will work really hard. Come on back here and understand, I'll give you one week to proof out. You understand?"

"Yes ma'am," the girl replied.

The old woman took the girl back to the kitchen where she was about to make bread. She gave her an apron. This was 1931, on Northwest 13th street in Oklahoma City. The girl was indeed fourteen years old and newly married. The girl was my mother. It was early summer, on a Monday morning at 5:30 a.m.

Miss Isle said, "You pay attention because starting tomorrow morning at 5:00 o'clock, this is yours to do. First thing."

Miss Isle already had put out a huge metal bowl that had 20 pounds of flour in it. She made a large indention in the center of the flour and turning the large bowl, gently pressed the flour against the walls of the bowl. Satisfied that she had a strong wall of flour around the bowl, she stepped over to the stove where a large pan of water was kept warm, four quarts, not too hot, not to cool, just right.

To the water she added sugar, salt, and four cakes of yeast. She stirred the mixture. She lifted the pan and gently poured the water into the well created in the flour. She then took a double handful of lard and placed it in the water, squeezing the lard between her fingers as though she were milking a cow until the lard was reduced to very small pieces.

Miss Isle gently moved her hand around the well inside the bowl, softly introducing flour into the liquid, again and again and again. After a while, as the mix started to thicken, Miss Isle backed away. "Child," she said to my mother, "this is where people make a mistake, the dough is starting to become a living thing and it needs to rest a minute."

While the dough rested, she checked on the other women in the kitchen. They were making fried chicken, pinto beans, and cobbler. She went out back to pay the man delivering milk. She came back over to the bread bowl and had my mother feel the mix. Then she continued. After a while, the mixture was quite thick and Miss Isle said, "The dough needs another rest," and she backed away.

"You have to respect the dough, honey. You have to respect what it's going through, what with all the things in it and with me pushing it around. Need to give it a rest now and again. It's kind of like people, you know. I want you to put your hands on it, not in it, but on it 'til I come back."

The warmth of the bread dough and the smell of ripe yeast became a part of my mother that day. Miss Isle came back, worked the dough a while longer, and then poured it out onto a well-floured table and lightly dusted it with more flour. She showed my mother how to knead the dough and left her alone to finish.

Lifting, pushing, kneading, and flouring a large amount of dough by herself gave my mother a confidence that stayed with her all her life. She proofed out that day.

Mike and Martha Larsen preparing for a holiday meal, complete with homemade bread.

It is a simple, but complicated thing to make bread.

Mother always made bread when I lived at home. But, of course, I never thought about watching her make it. It wasn't until I was much older that I had the good sense to have her teach me the art. What took her one day to learn, took me years. She understood the respect, I didn't. She understood the necessities of rest and gentleness and quiet. I didn't. I was always in a hurry. As she made bread she would say, "We should treat one another this way."

One of the things I have learned over my years as an artist is, painting is a lot like making bread. I build my own canvas and I do it carefully, gently. You can almost watch canvas breathe. I work with very good quality paint; it's an absolute pleasure. I am good to my tools for I know they will serve me well if I respect them. I have brushes that I have had for over twenty years because I care for them and treat them well. I have friends like that also.

Making bread was one of my mother's greatest pleasures. She was glad, as she grew old, that I had finally learned her secret and that I was passing it on to our children.

The secret of living.

The secret of being happy.

The secret of living life with respect for others.

The secret of success and fulfillment.

That I had finally learned...the secret of Making Bread.

Mike Larsen has mastered the art and continues the tradition of making bread.

Lela and Otto Carter, Larsen's grandparents, with the Chevy truck that Mike and his uncle delivered cattle in to the Oklahoma City Stockyards.

Juicy Fruit

1951

When I was little, I lived with my Grandma and Papa in Wynnewood, Oklahoma. Sometimes my uncle, a farmer and rancher, would take a load of calves up to the stockyards in Oklahoma City and take me with him. One morning, very early, he came by Grandma's and honked. Grandma had gotten me up and ready. I ran out and climbed up into the truck. It was still dark.

We drove up to the stockyards in Oklahoma City and my uncle backed the truck up to a loading chute. The load of calves were bawling something fierce and several of them were down so he had to get in with them and get them up. He was cussing something awful. I climbed up on the outside of the loading chute and watched as the animals went down into a holding pen. I could watch them through the spaces between the wooden rails. I reached in and jabbed one in the ribs. He returned the favor by squirting me with a giant load of green poop. It hit me on my left side and ran all the way down my overalls and into my shoe. I was a mess. I climbed down pretty quick. My pocket was full of poop. Yuck!

Uncle finished unloading, signed a clipboard, and got back in the truck. He was a mess too. He drove over to an area where they let you wash out the back of your truck with hoses and he spent about thirty minutes cleaning out the mess. He climbed back in, looked at me, and said, "Hungry, little man?" I told him I was starving.

We drove out of the stockyards, passing under those giant horns, drove about half a block, and parked at the curb. We got out and walked up an alley. We came to a door that had a light above it and he rang the doorbell.

Directly, a heavy man, with not much hair, opened the door and gave us both a good looking over. "I am covered from head to toe with cow shit but thought we might be able to set in your kitchen and get some breakfast" my uncle said. The heavy man smiled and said, "Friend, you boys made this place, ya'll come on in here."

I followed my uncle in, but we didn't stop in the kitchen. The man took us up front and seated us in the center of the room. He went over and spoke to a nice looking woman in a white dress. She had a pretty hanky in her shirt pocket and

A young Mike Larsen about the same time he made the memorable trip to the stockyards with his uncle.

a tiny white apron with green trim. She came over to our table and said to my uncle, "No need to order, I'm going to bring you two cowboys the best damned breakfast you ever had." And she did. She brought eggs and lots of bacon and biscuits with gravy and potatoes and three kinds of jelly.

After we finished, the heavy man came over and he and my uncle drank coffee and smoked cigarettes for a while.

Grandma had given me a stick of Juicy Fruit before we left her house that morning. I had put it in the pocket of my overalls. I thought it would be just the thing to finish off this fine breakfast so I tried to find it. My hand came out of my pocket with the stick of Juicy Fruit, but it was covered with wet, green, calf crap. Wet. Smelly. I wiped my hand on the leg of my pants and let the gum fall to the floor.

When we finally left that place. It was just starting to get light. We walked down the alley back to the truck. My uncle lifted me up into the cab. It was warm and smelled kind of like a garden. He climbed in, started the big truck, and lit a Chesterfield. I thought about getting into my pocket again then remembered that I had left the Juicy Fruit stick under the table.

Next thing I remember my uncle shook me and said, "Wake up Mike, we're home."

I think about that morning every once in a while. How nice that heavy man was and how kind the woman in the white dress with the pretty hanky who waited on us was, never mentioning how we looked or how bad we must have smelled. I do know it's one of the many, many reasons we live in Oklahoma.

Twelve or thirteen years ago, Martha and I came really close to moving to Colorado, New Mexico, or Wyoming—where artists live. We fortunately came to our senses.

So, what is it? Is it the heritage or the history? Is it the abiding desire of the people here to help one another and be generous? Can it be as simple as that? We know so many people here who consistently go out of their way to help others.

All you gotta' do is ask, friend.

"You boys made this place. Ya'll come on in here."

All those years ago, in the early 1950's, my uncle and I went to the back door of a place. We were both covered with cow shit and were just hoping to get breakfast, but the people there treated us like we were the finest, and cleanest, customers ever. That place that fed us was in Stockyards City. It was a café. It was the Cattleman's Café.

The stockyards in Oklahoma City about the time Mike Larsen went with his uncle to deliver a load of calves.

16

Cowboys and Indians

Early 1950's

Back when I lived with Grandma and Papa I had a really good time and I was happy. Sometimes my cousin Roy would be there and I had somebody to play with. Roy and I always played cowboys and Indians. For some reason, I was always the Indian.

I had a little feather headdress that Grandma had made for me. It had two green feathers, two red, and one yellow—all sewn onto a band that had buttons all around. I had a little leather vest that had once been a coat till I got too big and she cut the sleeves off. It had fringe and one tiny pocket. I had brown leather shoes that I wore to keep from getting stickers and I wore my Roy Rogers underwear. That was it. A real Indian for sure.

Roy wore a two-gun set that included a rubber knife and a little compass that always pointed west. He had a red cowboy hat and boots with pointy toes. We both kept candy cigarettes in the corners of our mouths like Papa.

In those days, Papa kept his wagon and some of the machines he used in a corner of the back yard alongside Grandma's garden. Sometimes, Papa was hired to use a particular machine that he owned. It was a sickle or mower. He used it to cut grain or hay. It was a long device that went both ways from a seat in the center. It cut with dozens of small blades that worked from a central control and lots of pulleys and belts.

This entire machine was pulled by Papa's two horses, Jake and Old Son of a Bitch. He always made me stay in the house when he hitched up the animals because, he said, sometimes the horses would bolt and jerk the machine around. I could get hurt. More than once he had to jump

Mike Larsen in his cowboy outfit outside of the hospital in Luling, Texas.

out of the way and one time he had to replace a shoe because he wasn't quick enough and one of the blades cut off the tip of one, barely missing a toe.

That machine was responsible for a number of three-legged dogs all around Wynnewood. Roy and I were respectful of that machine and stayed away from it. It was ugly and mean looking. It had its eye on us.

Roy and I played hard and fast. I was always on the run because, after all, I was the Indian. One afternoon, it was really hot, I was running, full out, from Roy. He was shooting at me with both cap guns and we were running behind Grandma's house. I tripped, flew, and fell . . . hard. I flew down with my arms out like Superman and landed on something hard and unforgiving. Rusty. Sharp. Mean.

I rolled with the punch and came up smiling. Roy was right behind me.

He was staring at me as his guns fell to the ground. He turned and ran toward the house yelling, "I didn't do it. I didn't do it."

He ran into the house and a couple of seconds later, here came Grandma running towards me, her hands waving above her head. She was shouting for my Papa, "Otto, Otto, come quick!"

I stood looking at her as she came towards me. I took a step and my right foot was sloppy in my shoe as if I had stepped in warm water. Papa came rushing out the back door banging the screen against the wall. I looked down and saw that from the knee down my right leg was covered in red, in blood, my blood. My shoe was full of my blood.

Before I could think, my Papa was there. He picked me up and wrapped his big hand completely around my leg and the wound on the side of my knee. The cut was only two inches long but when you consider that I was only three feet tall, that's a big cut.

In Papa's arms, off we went. The people across the road had a car and that's where Papa was headed. Grandma was running ahead of us with her skirt pulled up and when Papa and I got there, a man was coming out his front door and we all met at his car. It was a big black car. We all piled in, Papa still had his hand wrapped around my leg.

We got to the hospital in Wynnewood pretty quick and Papa carried me in. A nurse in a white dress saw us and yelled, "In here!" In we went, into a room with really bright lights. I was placed on a table that was cold. There was a lot of talking back and forth and Papa was cussing something fierce, then in *he* came.

In he came—a round man in a fine suit. He had rosy cheeks and not much more hair than Papa. "He" was Dr. Shelly, Wynnewood's most important citizen. He looked down at me, then at my Papa. After a few moments he put a small hand on Papa's shoulder and said, "Otto, you're going to have to turn loose so I can see what's going on."

Papa slowly unwrapped his hand from my leg. Blood was flowing from the wound. The doctor directed the nurse on what to do, as he got ready to sew me up.

It was as though I was watching the whole thing from somewhere else.

Papa had backed away from the table, his khaki shirt red on the front from my blood. He leaned against the wall, hands hanging at his side, and I noticed for the first time that he wasn't wearing his hat. My Papa never left the house, never, without that fine black hat. I had never seen him without it. But, in his rush to take care of me, he forgot it.

The doctor went to work on my leg saying things to the nurse that I didn't understand. Grandma kept her hand on my forehead. I wasn't scared and I didn't cry. I'm an Indian.

I looked up at the doctor and said, "When Papa told me we were gonna' come see you, it made me feel pretty good."

"Really?" the doctor said. "And why's that?" He kept casting an eye at my Papa as he worked on my leg.

In the past, he and Papa had never walked on the same side of the street, so to speak. The doctor was a strict Southern Baptist and went to church ten or twelve times a week.

Papa never went to church at all. Me and Grandma went to the church of Christ. But not Papa. That could have been the reason or it could have been the fact that Papa took a drink once in a while. Sometimes, more than one.

With streaks running down both sides of my face where tears had run through a thin layer of dirt I looked up and told him, "Papa said he never had to worry about Jake and Old Son of a Bitch because if they got sick he brought them to you because you were the best horse doctor around. I figured if Papa would let you work on those two, you ought to be able to work on me."

I don't know why but my Grandma nearly fainted and the nurse ran from the room holding herself like she had to pee real bad.

The doctor looked at Papa again, but this time with a thin smile, and said "Well, as horse doctors go, I guess I can hold my own."

After a while he finished up and had a conference with Grandma and Papa.

The nurse wheeled me out to the car in a wicker wheelchair and we went home.

Grandma put me to bed in their bed that had a feather mattress and I went to sleep pretty quick. When I woke up my leg was real stiff and hurt.

Sitting beside the bed in a straight back chair was my Papa. He was asleep. His chin was on his chest. He had not taken time to change his shirt and his big hands rested on his thighs, the left one still dark red from my blood.

He was wearing his hat.

I lay there looking at my Papa and fell into a nap. In my dream I was walking to town with Papa. I had on a headdress with red and green feathers and it was funny, but I only had one shoe. We were walking side by side and I reached up and took his hand, his big strong hand. It was red.

I felt safe.

Mike Larsen in front of the home he lived in with his grandparents in Wynnewood. Note Papa, left, looking on.

Mike Larsen's portrait of his grandfather was on display at one of his early shows, but was not for sale. A woman offered Mike $300 for the painting—$300 Mike needed. Mike agreed to sell her the painting only if she agreed to will the painting back to him if she were to pass away first. The agreement was honored and today the painting hangs in the Larsens' home.

THE UNDER

1950

"The only thing we have to fear, is fear itself." FDR

That...and the UNDER.

In the years I lived with my Grandma and Papa in Wynnewood, Oklahoma, I was able to spend a lot of time with my cousin Roy. He was the same age as me, older by a couple of months. His home was in Dallas, Texas, but my aunt brought him to Papa's house a lot it seemed like. Sometimes Roy would stay for a couple of weeks at a time.

I felt kind of bad for Roy. He cried a lot and, as I remember, was always in trouble. Quite often he got me in trouble as well.

There was a side building next to Papa's house that had once been a smoke house. It smelled like old meat. They called it the "Dog House." It had become an extra bedroom and was used mostly by another aunt of mine from Oklahoma City who had about a dozen kids and a very fat husband. The smoke house was where Roy and I slept.

Roy and I played cowboys a lot and he loved to go out back and throw rocks at Papa's two horses. I would always go set on the front porch swing and watch Papa sleep when that was going on.

My Papa was a fierce man, the biggest man I knew. He wasn't but about 5′7″ but he wore a very tall black hat that he kept brushed, no crease, very tall. I would watch him put it on very carefully, just so, with a slight pull to the right. He was fierce for sure but he was also very proud.

One afternoon, Papa was asleep in his chair on the front porch. Roy grabbed me by the shirt and said, "Come on, let's go play." He already had on his guns and boots and had a rubber knife in his belt. The only thing missing was a hat. He pulled me into the hallway. Hanging in its special place was a tall black, finely brushed hat. Roy grabbed it and, before I could speak, smashed a giant crease down the middle and put it on his head. It was way too big. He started for the front door.

Mike Larsen and his Papa, Otto Carter.

There Papa stood. He had just opened the screen door to come inside.

There we were, me and Roy. "You two little sons of bitches, what in God's name did you do to my hat?"

Roy threw the hat at me and ran for the back door. We didn't see him again for some time. I picked up Papa's hat and handed it to him. He took it, slowly pushed out the crease, smoothed over the top, and put it on. He cocked it and ran his hand over the top. It wasn't perfect, anymore.

He looked down at me and said, "Why didn't you run away, you little shit?" I couldn't come up with an answer. "Tell your Grandma I'll get lunch in town." he said as he walked out, slamming the screen door.

He left me standing there. I hated that. He always took me with him on the walk to town. He would take the time to stop and let me pick flowers and he never pulled away when I would reach up to hold his hand. He always took me. Not today.

Every day, when Papa would walk to town, he would go to the post office, stop somewhere for coffee, then set in front of Fergesons' and talk with all the other old men. He would walk home somewhere about dinnertime.

That very bright and hot afternoon Roy and I were in the kitchen with Grandma. She was mixing up a big bowl of cornbread batter. "You two go get some potatoes and get a bunch 'cause that whole gang from Oklahoma City is coming," she said.

The potatoes were under the house where it was cool...and dark as night.

We stood there. Me and Roy. "Mike. Roy. Go get them potatoes." We went out the screen and stood there, looking down the side of the house. There it was, a small black opening in the side of the house, at ground level.

We stood there until Grandma yelled at us again. Roy said, "I ain't goin' in there!" And off he went. I stepped off the porch and walked a little closer to the black opening. I stood for a while and looked at it, watching it breathe. I looked at it. The opening to the UNDER. I could hear Grandma in the kitchen. She was singing some song about a river.

It was hot and I didn't have anything on but my overalls. I had a smooth rock in my pocket and I took it out and studied it for four or five minutes. I heard the screen door squeak and Grandma yelled. "I'm goin'. I'm goin'," I croaked.

I stepped a little closer. A little closer. To the UNDER. My mouth was dry. I was almost to it. I could feel its breath. My heart was pounding. I know I saw something move in there.

A shadow moved over me.

I looked behind me to see the biggest man I had ever seen. Like a giant. The sun behind him. It was my Papa. He had a Lucky Strike Cigarette in the corner of his mouth.

"I been watchin' for a while, Mike, and I need for you to know, there ain't nothin' under there that can hurt you and you know that I'll be right here when you come out." He put his big hand on my shoulder and patted me twice.

I got down on all fours, closed my eyes, and crawled into the mouth of the beast, almost fearless because I was covered with my Papa's armor. A tiny knight. I had to go back three times to get enough potatoes. Papa helped me carry them in.

I was brave.

We didn't see Roy for a couple of hours. I don't know where he went but he smelled awful when he got back. Grandma stuck him in the tub.

Papa and I sat on the front porch after we had delivered the potatoes. I was on the swing and he was in his old brown chair. "You and me will walk to town tomorrow," he quietly said then drifted off into a nap. I sat there for a while and watched him sleep. I fell into a nap too.

When Grandma woke us for dinner, I had been dreaming of someplace dark that smelled like fresh dirt and of things that move but don't have any shape and a voice singing, "When we gather at the river...I'll be there."

"Wake up, Mike."

Why I Believe In Santa Claus

1949

I don't remember my first encounter with Santa Claus. I'm sure it was when I was a baby because Mother loved Christmas and always did the best for my brother and me.

I do have a memory of a small sled attached to seven plastic reindeer floating above my bed. It seems the eighth reindeer only had one leg. Mother had tried gluing the other three on but couldn't make them stay. That reindeer became an ornament for the tree, a magic ornament.

After the age of three there is something of a blank space in my memory. During that period, I was in the hospital in Dallas and in a rehabilitation center in Luling, Texas. I had contracted polio.

I think Santa was just on hold for a while, but I'm sure he still had my little name in his book. All the nurses at Luling dressed in white. There were lots of kids there. Lots of need for Santa Claus. I can still smell the Christmas tree they had there.

When I look at photos from that period, I think I fared pretty well. Lots of those kids that I can see in the background of some of those photos didn't fare the same. One girl who contracted polio the very same week that I did, if still alive, is a total quadriplegic, encased in a silent shell that will only be broken open when she dies. Maybe she thinks of Santa Claus, but she will never touch him or tug at his white whiskers.

I can walk. I can mow grass. I can throw a baseball. I can make love. Not all at the same time, of course. I can pretty much do whatever I want, and I can paint. I can paint, delicately holding a brush with these fine instruments called fingers, fingers that could easily have been ruined and worthless.

I remember Santa Claus. I grew up with him, this round man dressed in red. He is tucked away in my mind now because I am an adult, having put aside "most" childhood dreams.

Martha and I introduced our children to the wonderful world of Santa Claus very early and kept their excitement going for a wonderfully long time. The reindeer and sled that I grew up with now divided into separate ornaments adorning four trees each Christmas.

For a period of time, when I was small, I lived with my Grandma and Papa in Wynnewood. Mother was in Dallas where she could work. The last Christmas I was with them, Papa brought in a small tree and we all decorated it. The tree was just a little taller than me. The house smelled really good. Grandma was a very good cook. People came by, like my aunt and uncle. Even the doctor who fixed up my leg stopped by. He and Papa got along better now, even though he still considered Papa a heathen.

On Christmas Eve, even though it was warm and nice in Grandma's house, I felt kind of low. Papa knew why and assured me that Mother would be coming, sure as shootin'. On Christmas Eve night, it took me a long time to get to sleep.

When I woke up it was light. Mother was sitting beside my bed in a straight back chair watching me sleep. She had on a grey suit and a blue shirt. She picked me up and we hugged. She smelled like White Shoulders perfume. She had gotten on a bus at 10:00 p.m. when her shift was over at the restaurant and arrived in Wynnewood five hours later. She walked the eight blocks to Papa's house. We were together on Christmas Day.

After opening presents and having breakfast, I went outside. I was wearing a new little leather coat; it was light brown with fringe and one small pocket. It was an Indian coat.

When I came back in, Grandma had made me some hot chocolate. I took it and went to find Mother. I sat in a straight back chair and looked at her. She was lying on my bed. I sat on the chair for a long time, holding my chocolate, watching her sleep.

Santa Claus had come to our house.

Ruth Carter Larsen, right, worked in a club in Dallas, Texas. While in Dallas, Mike lived with his grandparents—Otto and Lela Carter.

Ruth Carter Larsen outside her café, Ruth's Café.

Ruth's Café

1956

Gourmet, it ain't.

My first job as an aspiring artist was peeling potatoes at my mother's cafe in Wynnewood, Oklahoma. I was twelve years old at the time. The year was 1956. Summertime. My first experience with art was at the café.

A man had come through town. He was a sign painter and convinced Mother that she needed a sign on her front window by the door. The sign would read, "Through this door pass the best people in the world, my customers."

He was a small man and had only one arm. He smelled kind of funny and had a fierce squint. He set about painting the sign. He set on a box and painted the words on the inside of the window, backwards. This was great! I found a gallon can in the kitchen and sat outside the window opposite him and watched every stroke he made. I don't think he liked that.

He had a cigarette in the corner of his mouth the whole time. I couldn't hear him, but I could see him mouth words. He was silently saying, "Why don't you go away, you little bastard." I watched until the sign was done. It took most of the morning.

An advertisement for Ruth's Café that appeared in the Wynnewood newspaper.

On the days I peeled potatoes, I would walk downtown to the café when I got up and Mother would fix me some breakfast. After eating I would hold out my hand and she would give me a dollar. I would walk down to the State Bank of Wynnewood, deposit my dollar, and get smiled at and pinched because I was so cute. Then I'd go back to the café and commence peeling about a thousand pounds of potatoes.

After I had peeled for about an hour, it would be lunchtime so I would set at a card table they had set up in the kitchen and Mother would bring me some lunch. Sometimes while I was eating, a colored man would come in the back door and sit with me at the card table. One of the cooks would bring him some lunch and we would eat together.

I knew some of these men and they would ask me, "You still peelin' taters, little one?" I liked these men. I asked Mother once why these men didn't eat up front like everyone else, she just told me to be quiet and eat my lunch.

Mother really worked hard at the café and pretty much the only time I saw her was at work. She left home before I got up and I was always asleep when she got home.

There were some really strange people downtown and I got to know them because I spent most of my time at the café, or close by. The barber was extra weird. I would climb up into his barber chair and he would always say, "You're gonna' look mighty strange you little son of a bitch if I accidentally cut off one of those big ears of yours." Each time I left, I always had to feel to make sure they were still there.

Main Street in Wynnewood while Ruth Carter Larsen owned and operated Ruth's Café. The café sign can be seen on the left side at the far end of the street.

The beauty shop, two doors down from the café, where Mother went to get her hair "did" was run by a large woman with big blond hair. Her hands were always colored red or blue or black. She had a big fight one day with her husband right in front of the beauty shop. He was a big hairy man. It seems that he had been watching television or something with the woman who ran the post office and got caught. He disappeared right after that. I don't know what went with him.

Every Saturday morning Mother would give me a quarter and I would go to the Deal Movie Theater to watch the movies. For twenty-five cents I got a ticket, a soda, a candy bar, and popcorn. The only thing we had to watch out for were the silly girls that just had to sit right behind us boys.

After Roy Rogers had saved thirty or forty people or Gene Autry had developed a bad cold, the movie would be over and we would run out of the theater. It would be a race to see if we could get out and run up the hill without getting kissed. Sometimes we made it. Sometimes we didn't.

I walked down the hill one day, it was just about lunchtime and there were several people sitting at the counter in Mother's café. They were all looking toward the kitchen. Standing in the doorway to the kitchen were Mother and my uncle. He had a big finger in her face and was actually yelling at her. "You let one of those Coloreds eat up here again, you better close your doors because I'll see to it that not another white person will come in here. Got me? "

That was my uncle. Mother's brother. The only man, besides my Papa, that I had. He was yelling at my mother. He stormed out the door.

Mother went into the kitchen. I followed.

She was leaning on the edge of the sink. I went up beside her, stood there for a few seconds, and asked her, "What's wrong, Mother?" She looked down at me, ran her fingers through my hair, and said, "Nothing for you to worry about, honey." Then she smiled at me. There were tears in her eyes.

Doing business in a small town can be difficult. It seems it always depends on how much a person is willing to compromise. Mother was not willing to compromise.

When my brother and I were living with Grandma and Papa, Mother was living in Dallas where she could find work. While she was there, she met a man who eventually became my stepfather. When Mother bought the café in Wynnewood, he stayed in Dallas but came to visit us on weekends.

I remember that no one in Wynnewood cared for him. He wore suits. He actually put cologne on his face. He smoked a pipe instead of a "roll your own." He talked funny. He never said "ain't" and he didn't care for the rodeo.

Things changed. I think it was largely because of my uncle that my mother and my new stepfather made the decision to sell Ruth's Café and move to Amarillo, Texas as I entered the seventh grade.

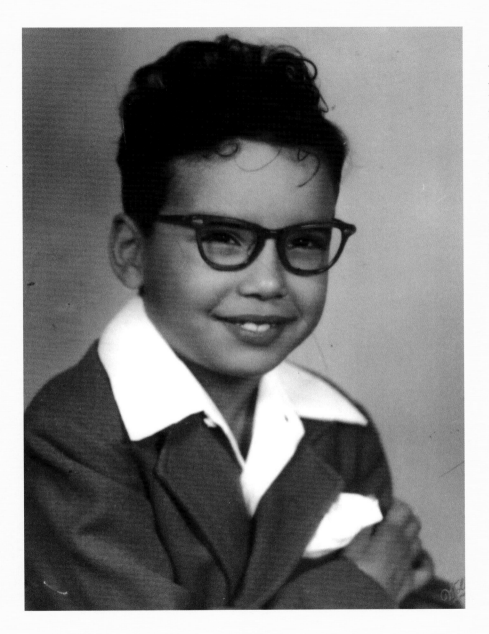

Ruth's Café was a big part of my life for a few of my younger years. I learned how to work and save money. I learned that kissing girls isn't all that bad. I learned that sometimes the people you look up to don't have the character you wish they had. I learned how to take care of myself because, generally speaking, no one else will. I learned to never allow compromise to cloud good judgment.

It's funny but I always said I'd never live in a small town again and have to take care of myself. Look at us now. We live in a small town just a teensy bit bigger than Wynnewood.

But now I have Martha.

Mike Larsen during the time his mother owned and operated Ruth's Café in Wynnewood.

CLASS IS AN ACQUIRED ACHIEVEMENT

In the years between 1978 or so and 1985, I taught a weekly art class. It was a reasonably easy way to make a few bucks and, as it happened, I actually enjoyed the experience.

I mention one of my students in another segment. I talk about his exceptional talent. I have wondered if he is still taking classes. He had talent but no confidence, no fire.

These classes were on a Tuesday night and I usually had ten to twelve students at any given time. Ages ranged from twenty to eighty and there were always more women than men. That was okay with me, men are usually not prone to listen to instruction.

As these classes were continual, there was no beginning class. Students would stay for a while then drop out and be replaced by new faces, new attempts at greatness. Once a month, I would do a demonstration and the crowd would be larger. Again, that was fine with me. I am an exhibitionist at heart.

Teaching a class with people who, with exceptions, don't have much talent, is a delicate situation. Early on, I hurt the feelings of a couple of people. I regret that, but I learned.

In 2005, Mike Larsen was the featured artist at Norman, Oklahoma's Mayfest.

In 2016, Mike Larsen spent the day at the Gaylord-Pickens Museum, home of the Oklahoma Hall of Fame, demonstrating his technique and the process of creating his works of art.

Once a month or so, we would have a nude model. The students would all chip in on the cost. There was a college nearby populated with young people who loved to take their clothes off. I had a waiting list of young students waiting to expose themselves, not that I minded. For no particular reason, I seemed to prefer female models, flowing hair, soft curves, and pink toenails. God help me.

Once in a while, though, I would have a young man model. Male models are "kind of like a box of chocolates, you never know what you're gonna' get." On one occasion, we had a young man model for us. He came in, disrobed, and struck a pose like the young David. He had done this before.

This was a drawing class and everyone had set up a board and taped up a large piece of drawing paper. The smell of charcoal dust was heavy. There was little or no conversation. Some of the students were actually looking at the model. There were eight women and two men in the class. One of the men was a Priest. He was very competent and quite talented. He had been a student of mine for a couple of years. I left him alone as he observed the model. After a while he approached his paper with flourish and produced quickly a fine, expressive, contour line drawing of the model from head to toe. Fantastic. Over the years, Martha and I purchased several pieces of his, mostly sculpture.

I watched him for a few moments, then moved down the line of students until I came to this one woman, fifty or so, tight hair, glasses, and wearing an apron with a pattern of kittens and a brown spot high up that looked like coffee had been spilled there. She was not looking at the nude male model and her face and body were so close to her paper I could not figure how she could possibly be drawing.

I said, "Ahem," and got her attention. I continued, "You might think about backing away from your pap..." I looked at the drawing. She had produced a drawing, a drawing of a man with no penis. My brain shut completely down. I had nothing to say. I moved on.

The next lady was always a concern. When she painted she would get paint all over herself, and anyone who happened to be close. She was around eighty. She also wore an apron, but it was difficult to identify the pattern because there would be so much paint on it. If I happened to get to her late in the class, she would be sitting in a chair unable to move. She would have a loaded brush stuck between each finger, unable to function.

I would take the brushes from her one at a time, and it would be as if I had released her from bondage. She would breathe deeply and say, "Oh, thank you, thank you." Over the years I learned a lot from these students. Some of them, unknowingly, had much to offer, maybe a touch with a brush, or a keen eye for color, or a flourish with a stick of charcoal.

I will say that one thing I did discover is that reality may be the realm we live in, but it is perception that drives us... and makes us crazy.

Mike Larsen's completed demonstration piece from his visit to the Gaylord-Pickens Museum.

Mike Larsen sketching and preparing for his first gallery show after returning to Wynnewood, Oklahoma.

THE DARK HOLE INCIDENT

1972

Back in the early 1970's, I had my first gallery show. It was at the Norman Wilks Gallery in Oklahoma City, Oklahoma. Norman had seen my paintings at a local festival. We talked and I went out to his gallery for a visit. I didn't have nearly enough work for a show so we agreed that in a year we would have the very first showing of work by Mike Larsen. The only problem was that I didn't have anyone to celebrate with. Martha was still years away.

For some reason I can't remember, or maybe just not having someone to consult with, I decided to move back to my hometown of Wynnewood, Oklahoma, for my year of preparation. There would be plenty of subject matter, I knew people there from my childhood, and living there would be reasonably cheap. So much for thinking.

I moved into the Eskridge Hotel on Main Street in Wynnewood. Three connecting rooms with a hot plate, an apartment-sized icebox, and a ten-inch television.

It turned out that the friends I had from long ago didn't identify with my particular profession. They mostly worked at the refinery or in the oil field and couldn't figure out just what it was I was doing. So, as it happened, I was pretty much alone in a very small town.

I did, however, have relatives there such as my aunt and uncle who farmed and ranched north of town. I spent a lot of time on their land sketching. Many paintings came from time spent doing drawings of their cows that crapped on me, ate my sketchbooks, and generally made me acquire a taste for chicken. I also learned that cows fart, a lot.

One day I had driven out to their place and stopped on the road to look at a large cottonwood tree that I had admired for a while. The tree stood about twenty yards in from the fence. I was in my "Andrew Wyeth" period at the time. I got out of my Camaro, grabbed my sketchbook, climbed the fence, and settled myself under the tree.

Looking up into the tree was marvelous with the abstract shapes and negative spaces created by the branches. I commenced sketching.

I was seated with my legs crossed, facing the road so I could keep an eye on my car. I had done three or four sketches when I heard the truck coming. My uncle was in the truck and glanced at me as he passed. He drove by and slowly came to a stop. He backed up and stopped again, by my car. He leaned out the open window, looked at me, and said, "Whatcha' doin'?"

"I'm just drawing a picture of this tree," I said.

"You planning on being there long?" he asked.

"Don't know," I replied.

"Well, if I was you, I might get a move on." Having said that, he folded himself back into the driver's seat, put it in gear, and drove off.

How strange, I thought.

Mike Larsen's Uncle Floyd. It was on Uncle Floyd's land that Larsen prepared for his first gallery show.

I looked back up into the tree and continued my drawing.

I suddenly felt a heat on the back of my neck and something wet and nasty kept hitting me. There was a huffing sound I couldn't identify. I turned my head around and looked into the face of the biggest beast from hell I had ever seen. This Brahman Bull was no more than two feet behind me looking directly down at my head. Every time he exhaled, he blew my hair back and I could smell the sour stench of digested grass and sulfur. His eyes were black as hell and there was a wound near his nose dripping something vile.

We were on the field of battle, and without any effort, I had already lost.

I slowly rose to my feet. The time it took me to race, jump the fence, and get into my car couldn't have taken more than two seconds. When I looked back, the bull was slowly eating my sketchbook. Damned cows. When I went to my uncle's house the following Sunday for dinner, there was no mention of the incident. I did notice, however, that when I looked at him he would not meet my eyes. Damned uncles.

After many months of sketching on the farm and putting up with cows, I had produced enough paintings for a reasonably good show. I had been sending the works to a framer in Oklahoma City and he had been taking them to the gallery. As we got close to the show date, I spent time with Norman's assistant going over titles and prices. He assured me that he would hang the show well and properly title each painting. He had my list and I was confident there would be no type-os.

If I may interject here—as an artist, have confidence in yourself and your abilities. Have faith and be positive. You can rely on yourself, everyone else is suspect. Above all, don't take yourself too seriously.

Quite a number of people came to see the show. I was surprised. I'm sure it helped that Norman had a free bar and lots of food. I wandered through the gallery shaking hands and, awash with light praise, was not offended by the occasional snicker or covered smile.

Most of the paintings were smaller in size with one exception; on the very back wall was the biggest work. It was a large pastoral scene of a herd of my uncle's Black Angus cows gathered around a watering hole. I remember thinking, "I wonder what cows talk about around the watering hole?" I know what the two black bulls on the hill are talking about. But, that's another story, for another time.

I had never been good at naming my paintings, so the name of this large work was simply *Black Angus*. Descriptive, at least.

The show ran its course and the night ended. I had some sales, not enough to cover my framing bill, but what the hell. As people left, they were all smiles and some slapped me on the back saying things like, "Hell of a sense of humor you got, Mike."

Okay.

As nearly everyone had left I wandered back to check sales and finally came to the large painting. I knew it hadn't sold but looked down at the title and price tag anyway. He misspelled it! The sorry son of a bitch misspelled it! My mouth went instantly dry and I thought I was dropping down a large dark hole. Deeper and deeper.

The title of the painting, spelled out in all capital letters, the cause of snickers all night, the covered smiles I didn't understand, and the slaps on the back. All came clear— BLACK ANUS the card said. BLACK ANUS was the title of my best painting. I kept looking for the "g" but it was nowhere to be found.

I had relied on someone else.

BLACK ANUS. BLACK ANUS.

A dark hole indeed!

Mike Larsen's largest piece of work at the Norman Wilks Gallery was *Black Angus*.

43

Oh, What Big Hands You Have

1969

In the late 1960's I went to the University of Houston for a year to study with a nationally-known sculptor that was only going to be teaching there for one semester. Mostly what I remember about him is that each day he would just look at this group of aspiring sculptors, shake his head, and chuckle.

I learned what I know about sculpting from that class so long ago and I apply it today, even though at the time I thought I was learning nothing.

Mike Larsen's "signature" is oversized hands in his work.

Side note:

We had a model for that class, a German girl who spoke no English. She was a short, but large girl with pendulous breasts. She loved to take her clothes off.

At the instructor's direction she would strike her pose and remain unmoving until the break. At the word "break" she would unfold, stretch, and head for the door.

The art department at the time was three army barracks connected together to form a long building with a long hall running through all three. Our sculpture class was the first class of building number one. Looking out our door you could see down the hall all the way to the end of building number three.

Our German model would start at our door, in the nude, and do cartwheels all the way to the end of building number three, turn around, do cartwheels all the way back to our room, throw her arms up high, say something loudly in German, go to the bathroom, and resume modeling.

Interestingly, because we were all used to her, we didn't pay much attention. But, looking down the hall, you could see all the doorways with dozens of students' heads sticking out, watching her go by.

She was a sight to behold.

I digress.

This instructor had us continually study the sculptors of the past, in particular Michelangelo and Rodin. These two tended to make the hands of their subjects just a little large. In Michelangelo's case, the young David is an example.

We all took this to heart and produced many pieces with larger than necessary hands. That effect seemed to naturally become an essential part of my paintings over the years.

If it was good enough for Michelangelo, it is certainly good enough for me.

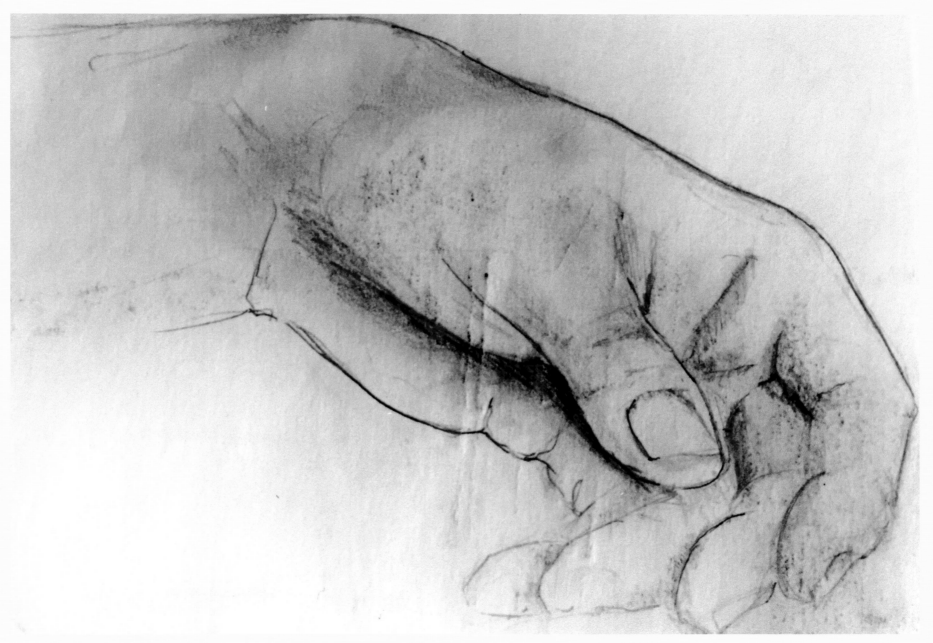

A sketch of one of many of Mike Larsen's oversized hands used in his work.

The works created by Mike Larsen in the 1970's is different from the Native American genre he is known for today.

Jurassic

1977

Eighty Million B. C. Give or take.

The only really dry land was atop what is now Black Mesa. All the surrounding area was covered with marshes, wet lands, and very nasty creatures. A large creature with three mighty horns grazed at the base of the Mesa.

The Triceratops was not a mean animal. He pretty much kept to himself, trying to avoid trouble. Kind of reminds me of . . . me. He would go through his days not really accomplishing anything, not spending too much time in thought, because his brain was so small and prone to trivial concerns. Is that me again? Finding food and an accommodating female was of utmost importance. The other creatures paid him small notice, maybe because he didn't look especially tasty or because he seemed to be aggressively "horny" all the time. Ah, the similarities persist.

The days came and went, one pretty much like the next, until it came time for the big beast to mingle with the stars, the only evidence of his having been here, a fragment of bone.

Hard to say, but perhaps the spirit of that great animal stayed in the wind of western Oklahoma for millions of years and finally noticed, coming up the trail from the east, a strange looking beast with short round legs and eyes like a giant dragon fly, passing fumes like one of the many oil pit fires. A yellow and brown concoction. Another dinosaur for sure. A 1972 Volkswagen bus.

In the summer of 1977, an artist friend and I drove out to Guymon, Oklahoma for a weekend art show. The thinking being that they had little to do in Guymon so the show would be well attended. Oh, well.

My friend had made a call to a buddy of his who worked on a ranch in the far western county of the Oklahoma panhandle to see if we could come out to camp and paint on the ranch after the show was over. His buddy said it would be fine as long as we didn't bother the cows and promised to leave the goats alone. When the show ended, off we would go.

On our way out to Guymon we passed through the tiny town of Slapout. You could look out the side window of the bus to the south and see Texas about a hundred yards away. We stopped at a filling station that had a café and curio shop attached. There was an old man sitting in a lawn chair by the door watching us as we got out of the bus.

I pulled the handle from the gas pump and commenced filling the tank. My friend went on inside the store. The old man just kept watching.

Tank full, I put the handle back and turned to go in.

"You best have cash, we don't do credit." the old man said.

There was a very round Indian woman behind the counter who took my money. She wasn't very tall and had on a shift with a floral print pattern. Her skin was perfect, but her hair was pulled back so tight I didn't see her blink her eyes the whole time we were there. There was the smell of pinto beans cooking in the air.

I didn't hear him come in, but when I turned around the old man was standing right behind me. He was wearing khaki from head to foot and the toe of his right boot was taped all around with duct tape. He wore a ruined brown hat with a leather band and he kept a cigarette at the corner of his mouth, smoldering. His eyes were both rheumy and

During the 1970's, Mike Larsen's work leaned more towards cowboys and ranching.

difficult to look at. I couldn't think of anything to say, so I just stood there.

"I got something I bet neither one of you two sons 'o bitches has ever seen, if you're interested."

"Sure," we said in unison.

"It'll cost you a dollar each." We both whipped out a dollar.

"Foller me," he said.

Back in those days, I didn't carry a pistol.

He led us through a doorway, down a hall, and through another door where he turned on a huge bank of lights. We walked into a museum. It was a large metal building attached to the back of the café.

"Well, what do you two think of that?"

We were looking at row after row of absolutely beautiful antique cars, mostly black but with some exceptions, like the yellow 1932 Ford convertible. They were all polished and shone in the overhead lights. The smell of polish was rich in the air. The old man's eyes were suddenly bright.

"Back in the '30's, me and my daddy would take a team out west of town and every few days we would find one of these cars and pull them back here. They're mine now." He smiled. All his teeth, upper left, were missing.

In those horrible days of the Dust Bowl, people with little hope would head west and have to abandon their cars when the gas ran out. Their plight and bad fortune became an opportunity for an enterprising old man and his son.

We left there that day not really understanding the feeling of loss, of emptiness.

Before we left Guymon, the show behind us, we stopped at a Safeway and stocked up on camp food, which included three cases of Budweiser, and off we went. We had directions for where to turn into the ranch. It was about five miles before the state line.

Because I consider myself reasonably intelligent, I knew right off we had gone too far when I saw the sign, "ENTERING NEW MEXICO." We backtracked two miles to the little town of Kenton and pulled up to the only store in town. I got out and spoke to an old man sitting in an old green lawn chair by the door. It seems that somebody had made a fortune passing through this country selling lawn chairs.

I asked directions to the ranch entrance we had missed. The old man squinted up at me and said, "Well, you two boys are sure as hell lost. Tell you what." He pointed east with his chin. "Go back a few miles and keep your eye out on the north side of the road. When you see a dinosaur bone tied to the fence, that's where you turn in. The ranch will be a few miles up."

We headed east, kept our eyes out, found the bone, and turned in. We stayed on the ranch for a few days and had a pretty good time. We painted a few paintings, drank all the beer, and went home.

As we left the ranch, I got out of the bus at the entrance to study the bone tied to the fence with baling wire. The past reached out and touched me. I looked around at the dry, bleak landscape trying to visualize what it might have been like when this animal walked around here. No way, Jose. Black Mesa shimmered in the distance. I climbed back in the bus and off we went, back to the present.

We are all a part of the history of this great Earth. The people we have met and will meet, the experiences we have had and will have, will become a part of each of us. We must absorb our history, knowing that our souls will be enriched by the history we share.

History will always reach out to touch us and the journey will never stop until finally we all mingle with the stars singing praise to God.

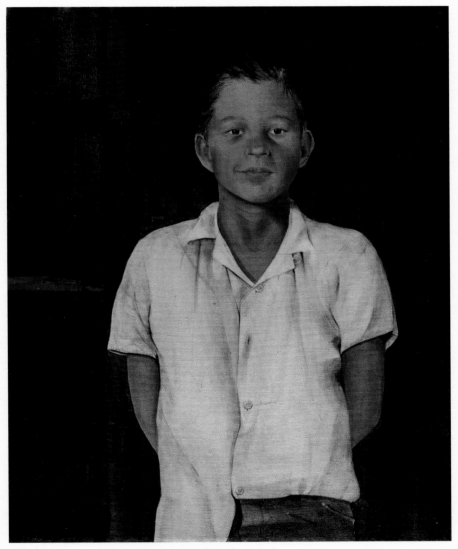

Mike Larsen's work during his Andrew Wyeth-period.

Mike Larsen's work from the 1970's.

THE CRITIC

1969

In 1969 I was attending the University of Houston and one day on a whim I wrote Peter Hurd and asked if I could come out for a visit and have him critique some of my paintings. I followed that up with a phone call and his wife Henriette Wyeth, sister of Andrew Wyeth, answered. She said "Mawvelous dawling, you just come on out." So I did.

I put several paintings in the back of my 1968 Chevy and off I went.

I finally arrived in San Patricio, New Mexico, where he lived. I asked around, received directions, and found his compound west of town.

It was a beautiful place—high walls, stucco buildings within, and hand-carved gate. I drove in and went to the main house. Didn't get to meet Henriette, she was napping. A servant gave me directions to Peter Hurd's studio across the yard.

I walked over to the studio and stood at the open door for a few seconds, watching the artist at work on a rather large painting. Directly he noticed me and motioned me to come in.

Hurd worked in egg tempera, a difficult method of using egg yolk mixed with water and dry pigment. Makes me tired.

We talked for a few minutes and I reminded him of why I had come.

"Come over here and sit," he said. We moved to a corner of his studio and sat in front of a large open fireplace.

"Let me tell you a story," he said, "about critics. Couple of years ago I was working on a series of paintings right here in this studio. I was finishing up on one of the last of the paintings. I had a large dog at the time, a German Shepherd, about 115, 120 pounds, big dog. She hung around the studio usually in front of this fireplace. Anyway, it was about midday and someone hammered the dinner bell and I went in for lunch.

"I leaned the painting I was working on up against the wall and went in to eat. Had my lunch and a short nap and came back out here to finish that painting. I walked in the studio door and unbelievingly looked at my painting, which was leaning against the wall, the dog sitting in front of it smiling like a raccoon, her face colored like a rainbow. She had licked off the entire bottom half of my nearly finished painting. My brain was on fire.

"I ran over and grabbed the dog by the neck and tail and carried her outside. She was a big dog. I was determined I was going to throw her down the well. I got her over by the well and stood there. Unmoving. I looked back at the studio and dropped the dog and ran back inside. I stood looking at the painting leaning against the wall. My mouth dropped open and I said, 'My God, the dog was right.'

"I grabbed some charcoal and began redrawing the foreground of the painting. I was lost in thought when one of my workers rushed in the door yelling, 'Patron, Patron, the dog ees in the well.'

"We ran out to the well and sure enough there was the dog at the bottom.

"One of the boys had thrown down a rope hoping to lasso the dog. He finally did get the rope around the dog, around her neck. Three of the boys commenced pulling the dog up. By the neck. She was a big dog. I looked down and you could see the dogs eyes were all bugged out. There was a strange grin on her face and her front paws were together as though she were praying.

"I could almost read her thoughts...'what'd I do, what'd I do... my master tried to drown me now these Vaqueros are trying to hang me...what'd I do?'

"They were finally able to pull the dog out and she flopped down on the ground and just laid there. We watched her for a while then I went back to work. One of the boys said later that the dog finally got up and just wandered off. A couple of days later I was working on the painting and happened to glance around and there she was lying in front of the fireplace, looking at me. Every time I would look her way, she was watching me. This went on every day for months.

"I tried over the years to get her to comment on other paintings, but she wouldn't have any of it. That's the way it is with critics. They're at their best when they're quiet."

With that, he stood up and said, "Now, if you don't mind, I need to get back to work."

We said our goodbyes and I left and drove home. He never did look at my paintings, but I think he gave me what I needed. I have never again to this day asked anyone else for criticism of my work.

During this period in Mike Larsen's career, he began experimenting in the style of Andrew Wyeth, saying "Everyone was trying to paint like Wyeth."

A still life painted by Mike Larsen after his visit to New York.

NEW YORK, NEW YORK
WHEN YA' GOTTA' GO, YA' GOTTA' GO

1984

Going to New York City for an Oklahoma boy is kind of like swimming in a really cold lake. You have to just put fear aside and jump in. There is no way to attack that town gradually.

In the early 1980's I had been doing street shows and festivals for a number of years. I remember that at every show after I had set up, I would move away from my display to judge the overall effect. It seemed that, more often than not, I would be overcome with a feeling of a need for advancement somehow.

What was missing?

I spent a few days at our museums trying to understand what the problem was and then it came to me. I believe while I was studying Thomas Moran at the Cowboy Hall of Fame in Oklahoma City, known today as the National Cowboy and Western Heritage Museum, what I was totally overlooking was very simple. Paint quality. A problem with young artists is that they tend to not think about what they are doing. It's easy to overlook the "how" while you're all wrapped up with the "how many." Don't get me wrong, I do recommend thinking for artists, on a limited basis, of course.

An artist should question his art always.

"Am I watching my design?"

"Are my colors cooperating?"

"How is my brushwork?"

"How is the quality of my...paint?"

Quality of *my* paint. Paint quality.

That sent me to New York.

My favorite artist is Edgar Payne. I could sit and stare at his paintings all day, and I have, because the paint is alive on his canvas. Paint quality.

I went to New York to study at the Art Students League on 57th just east of Broadway because a good friend of mine, Dick Goetz, recommended it. My first surprise on arriving in New York was paying cab fare of $30 for the ride into the city from the airport.

My second surprise happened as I was walking down Broadway. A beautiful woman was suddenly walking beside me, very close beside me. She was really tall. She looked down at me and said, "I can show you a really good time." My mouth was suddenly very dry as I looked up at her and said, "Ma'am, I'm from Oklahoma." She smiled and chuckled and said, "Well, maybe some other time," and she walked on by. I do remember watching her walk away.

At the Art Students League I studied with several instructors I had long admired. They were teaching me what I needed.

My adventures in New York don't really apply here except that I ate the best Italian food I ever had in my life. I ate squid, I think. Fantastic! I may have had too much Scotch.

The still life painted while Mike Larsen studied at the Art Students League remains in the author's private collection.

When I arrived home from this adventure in New York, I was so glad to get back to the Jesus is Lord Studio and Pawn Shop. My head was so full I don't believe I touched a brush for two weeks.

However, the first painting I did on my return was in the manner of one of my instructors and it turned out quite well. We still have that painting in our bedroom. Several paintings after that were crap. I was thinking too much.

I was a good painter when I went up there and would be an improved painter...in a while. Processing and absorbing and applying what I had learned to what I could already do was like trying to make a cake out of a cake that was already made. I had to discover how to utilize what I had learned and apply it to what I could do now and discard the rest. I didn't want to paint like any of the people I had studied with, but I know that if I had stayed longer I might not have been able to resist the temptation. I'm not necessarily weak, but have been known to take advantage of easy opportunity.

I was not after a style. I was after an understanding of application and how to include that into what I was already doing. At my age and weight, coming back to Oklahoma with a different style of painting than when I left would have been a disaster.

One thing I have discovered over the years is that art patrons look for several things in the artists they buy. They look for growth, certainly, but mostly they look for consistency. They may be willing to overlook the fact that artists tend to have a poor memory, but they will not forgive too many changes in the way an artist paints.

It was a risky thing, going to New York, but extremely beneficial. I still apply things that I learned there and have improved because of the experience. One of the best things in New York was the Metropolitan Museum of Art. Visiting with Van Gogh will educate me until I die.

As a side note, at the Museum it seemed that some of the nude Greek male statues had the shiniest balls. I watched for a while as people would go by and give those rascals a rub. Over the years, they had become quite bright.

Well, why not?!

I guess now I can truthfully say I helped polish the balls of history.

Above and facing page: Martha and Mike Larsen on their honeymoon at Rocky Mountain National Park.

Getting High

When Martha and I were going together, and after we married, we loved to camp out in the mountains of Colorado. More specifically, Rocky Mountain National Park.

One of the best things about camping out is that it's nearly as cheap as staying at a Motel 6, but without having close neighbors doing rude things to one another that you can hear.

On one of our camping adventures we were situated next to a Japanese man who swept his site clean every evening then sat on his camp table, cross-legged, and prayed. Impressive to say the least.

While we were in that campsite, we kept looking to the west and seeing an area of brightness atop a mountain. A glacier. I think that was the morning we discovered that boiling water for coffee was problematic because of the altitude, so we had Scotch instead.

We went into Estes Park later that morning and found maps of trails accessible, and sure enough, found a map showing the trail up to the glacier we had been seeing.

Off we went.

The only hiking equipment we possessed was desire and determination.

Finally arriving at the trails' starting point, we stopped to assess. We had a plastic gallon of water, two Milky Way bars, and a nagging feeling that we should go back to Estes Park and go to the movies.

Up we started. I had slipped my belt through the handle of the plastic bottle of water and we had eaten the two Milky Way bars. Martha was the path finder. I would follow her anywhere.

People kept passing us by, snickering or laughing out loud, healthy looking people in good shoes and shorts, with fanny packs and canteens. I had developed a limp on my right side from the weight of the gallon of water.

Up we went. We were determined.

After four hours, the landscape changed as we ascended the mountain, finally reaching the tree line. All of a sudden it was as though we were on the Moon, nothing green, only rocks. The only things growing here were the blisters on my feet, inside my Keds. The bottle of water was now only half full. We could see the glacier in the distance. We were determined.

As we looked up, the bright blue sky changed right before our eyes. Suddenly there were thick, snotty looking clouds and the temperature dropped at least thirty degrees in the time it took to take a breath. People in those wonderful shoes were running past us, in the other direction, down the mountain.

"What the...!" A young man with an accent yelled at me as he ran by, "WHITE OUT, WHITE OUT!" We could no longer see the glacier, or anything else, for that matter.

We turned and ran. Down. What took us four hours to attain, took less than an hour to undo. We got to the car and looked up. The entire mountain was gone, smothered in a

Mike, Martha, Kate, Jeffrey, and Randall on one of their many family camping trips at Rocky Mountain National Park.

dense cloud of frothy, freezing, white. Martha and I were covered with a light coat of snow.

Taking your kids camping is a whole 'nother animal. There is no TV, no Game Boy, and no phones. What there is, however, is a continual stream of complaints. Our oldest son was around twelve at the time. As it happened, he stayed twelve until he was nearly thirty. That's another story. Our middle son, even though he whined a lot, proved to be agreeable, up to a point. We always called him the "Cruiser." Still do.

Our daughter was continually finding things, things she just had to keep, like feathers or stones or sticks. One rock she found at the top of a mountain hike she had to have. The rock weighed in at twelve pounds or better and she just had to have it. I succumbed to tears, a quivering lip, and a long "Pleeeze, Daddy" and carried the damned thing all the way down the mountain.

I moaned and wheezed a lot back then, but looking back now, I remember, with gratitude, the adventures we had, the things we saw. Listening to elk sing in the morning mist still rings in my ears. Eagles gliding by and watching chipmunks eat our peanut butter caress my memory. Eating t-bone steaks cooked over an open fire and having to finish our meal, with whining kids, in the tent because of a sudden rainstorm, makes me pause.

Memories like these keep me safe, safe within the folds of my family, safe from becoming too overwhelmed by the daily business of living. Safe, as I continue this adventure... with the only woman I will ever love.

A family vacation in 1995.

Mike Larsen's drawing of Bobby Kennedy was done during the time he was leasing studio space from The Jesus Is Lord Pawn Shop.

THE JESUS IS LORD PAWN SHOP

1981-1991

The sign at the pawn shop read:

> We will Pawn your goods
> We will Buy your goods
> We will Pray for you
>
> But if you steal anything
> We will shoot you

The young man entered the pawn shop and casually looked around.

There were three men behind a long glass counter and another sitting at a very cluttered desk. The owner, an old man in his seventies, was facing the back wall taking inventory and writing in a large book.

The young man walked up to the glass counter. One of the men behind the counter said, "What can I do for ya' bud?"

The young man's eyes widened as he pulled a small, black .22 pistol from under his shirt and pointed it at the man. "I want all your cash money, quick." He was loud and sweat poured from his forehead.

In less than a second, the young man started shaking all over as he held the air he had just sucked in. There were five pistols pointed at him. All cocked. He turned and ran for the door. He yanked it open. His car, a 1969 Crown Victoria, was right there, motor running. He did a sliding vault across the hood. There was screaming behind him. He yanked open the driver's door and got in. He was "ROCKET MAN!"

The old man stood in front of the car.

The windshield suddenly exploded as 9mm bullets poured through. All the other men were filling the side of his Crown Vic with holes. No more windows.

The young man screamed. He jammed the car into gear and peeled out. He felt a heavy thump as he squealed onto Northwest 23rd Street.

All five men had emptied their 9mms and 45s into the escaping Crown Vic, the only injury, however, was to the old man. He was hit by the car as the young man sped from the lot.

All told, sixty or seventy bullets were fired into the car. No one was hit. Shepherd Mall was just across the street and several cars sustained broken windows and a hole or two in the body.

Mike Larsen in his studio owned by The Jesus is Lord Pawn Shop in northwest Oklahoma City.

The police pulled that uncontrollably shaking young man from his Crown Vic a few blocks away. His getaway car had died in the middle of the street, leaking fluids like a sieve.

They carried the old man away in an ambulance to Baptist Hospital where he was x-rayed and found to have no broken bones. They did, however, have to address the deep bruise across his abdomen, a bruise oddly in the shape of the grillwork of a 1969 Crown Victoria.

In the early 1980's, I finally got tired of painting in my garage and went looking for actual studio space. At the corner of Northwest 23rd Street and Villa Avenue, just across from Shepherd Mall, was The Jesus is Lord Pawn Shop. Attached to the shop on the south side was a large two-story building. The owner of the pawn shop owned the entire building. The downstairs part of the two-story building contained a ceramic store. Upstairs on the west side were apartments. The east side, upstairs, was one large empty room. Vacant. A sign was on the door. "Space for Rent." I took it. My landlord was the owner of the The Jesus Is Lord Pawn Shop.

I kept that studio for a number of years. The rent was good. It had good north light and was very large.

Over the years, the pawn shop would call me when some Indian would come in and sell an old head dress or a beaded fan. The old man who owned the shop didn't want to keep such things, as he was very superstitious. I built up quite a collection of artifacts which all hung in the studio.

While in that studio, I made a couple of good friendships with nationally-known artists who used my place to teach classes when they came to town. I studied with one of them when I went to the Art Students League in New York.

It was while I was using the "Jesus is Lord" studio that I met Martha.

One of the festivals that I had been in for a number of years was the Festival of the Arts in downtown Oklahoma City. I was there one afternoon at my booth when a mutual friend brought her by to introduce us. Martha had a picture framing business and I needed a framer. She had curly hair, was wearing blue and white shorts, had shining eyes above a field of freckles, and no makeup. No lipstick. She had the loveliest smile I've ever seen on a woman.

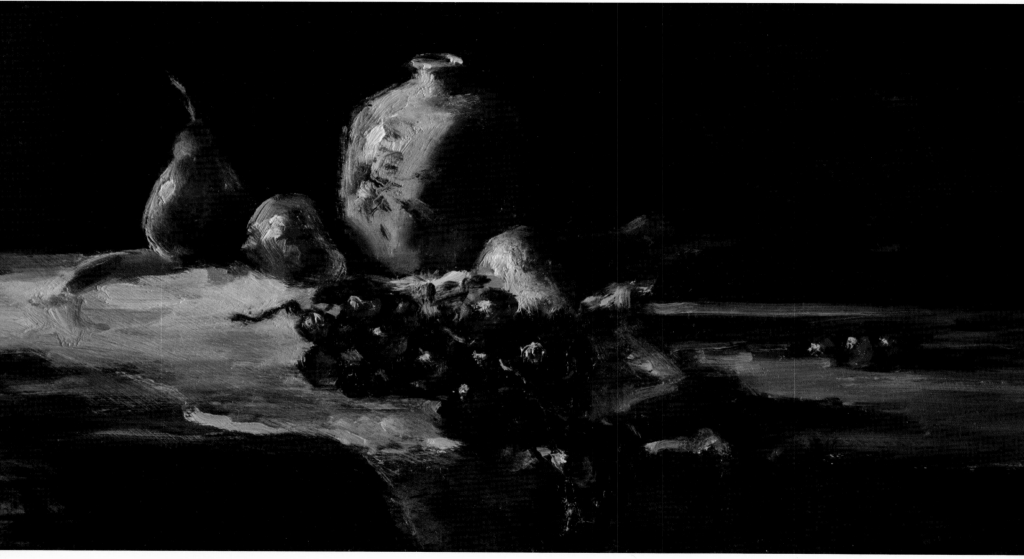

Still in the author's private collection, this still life is one of the pieces completed while Mike Larsen was renting studio space in northwest Oklahoma City.

I was struck by lightning. I do remember how much I enjoyed watching her walk away.

I was still in that studio when Martha and I married.

I have learned to enjoy this constant adventure, I will appreciate each day and the beauty within it.

The adventure will continue.

We will Pawn your goods
We will Buy your goods
We will Pray for you

If you steal anything
We will shoot you

We will shoot at you anyway.

Mike Larsen and Martha Schroeder, prior to their marriage, at an annual event hosted by Presbyterian Hospital in Oklahoma City.

Tony Roma's

1988

Success is fifty percent mental and ninety percent showing up...awake.

In 1988, or so, I met a gallery owner at the Prix de West show in Oklahoma City. His gallery was in Scottsdale, Arizona. I had sent him photos of work and we had agreed to talk at the Oklahoma City show. It all worked out and we ended up sending work to Scottsdale. I was really excited, as this was our first "big-time" gallery.

A few months later, the gallery called to see if we could get more work to them and to tell us that a national art magazine had seen our things and wanted to talk to us about possibly doing an article. We worked it out and agreed that Martha and I would bring work out on a certain date and the gallery owner, the magazine people, and Martha and I would all go out to dinner and discuss an upcoming article.

At the time, the car I had was a small mini van. I don't care to remember the make. The van had a habit of coughing and wheezing and when catching its breath would sometimes come to a complete stop, lifeless for a half hour or so. It did have a good radio.

Off we went, to Arizona.

The trip from Oklahoma City to Scottsdale usually takes two days, eight hours to Albuquerque and seven or so on to Scottsdale. We determined, however, to make it in one day, fifteen hours. We left the house in Oklahoma City at 3:00 a.m., heading west.

The trip was uneventful as we passed through the No Man's Land around Amarillo and on into New Mexico. The van would cough once in a while but it wasn't until we turned south at Holbrook, Arizona, and encountered the mountains that I realized how truly crummy the van really was. For the next sixty miles it died every ten minutes and we sat on the side of the road for a half hour until it was rested. We pulled into Scottsdale three hours later. We had been on the road for sixteen hours as we pulled up to the gallery. Our eyes were glazed over as we walked in.

The owner of the gallery welcomed us and said we were to meet the magazine people at the restaurant in about half an hour. "Mike" the owner said, "how would you like a very small drink before we go over, I have some really fine Scotch?" I greedily accepted. I took a drink.

After about five seconds Martha looked at me with one eye, the other was closed, and said, "You okay?"

"Oubuft." I said.

"What?"

"Mjuskay," I responded. Something was dreadfully wrong with my tongue.

The owner of the gallery came over and propelled us out the front door for the short walk to the restaurant, Tony Roma's. We walked into Tony Roma's and a pretty woman, with two heads, escorted us to our appointed tables. I correctly chose the one on the right. Four men stood up and one of them thrust a hand at me and said his name. "Mkliklarm," I replied and shook his arm vigorously.

We sat.

We were seated at a large round booth, I was on one side and Martha was on the other. Several men were sitting between us. It is still unclear what happened next, but I was looking directly at Martha. She was like a tree in the forest that had just been chopped off at the roots. I watched as she, very slowly, leaned then gently fell into a resting position on her side on the seat. She was sound asleep.

All the men were looking at her. One lost his pipe and it fell to the floor.

"Marma," I said.

"ZZZZ," she replied.

Lucky for us all, God watches over drunks and sleepyheads. It seemed that the publisher and editor of that magazine were quite amused and far from offended; we got the article in their publication. It seems *that* dinner is often talked about to this day.

I don't remember much about the meal except it was the best Chinese food I ever had in my life, I think. It seems like we ate for hours.

We just let Martha sleep.

ACES 'N EIGHTS

1987

You never touch another man's wife. More important, you never touch another man's hat. The most important thing of all though is, you never touch another man's cards.

The show was all set. We had sent down all the paintings. All we had to do, was show up.

The gallery was in San Antonio, Texas. A really fine gallery along the River Walk. It was winter and cold out and we were looking forward to being in the warmth of south Texas. It would be a full day's drive, but an easy drive. Interstate 35 south all the way.

It was raining when we left Oklahoma City with a flake of snow every once in a while. It was barely light as we started and should arrive in San Antonio mid-afternoon.

At the time, we didn't have iPhones or iPads. We had to rely on television weathermen for the forecast. I can count on one hand how many times they have been right about anything in the last year. Now was not one of those times.

By the time we got to Pauls Valley, it was snowing. When we arrived at the state line, it was a blizzard. We crept into Gainesville, Texas and pulled into a truck stop to make a phone call.

The high school graduation picture of Flonnie Schroeder, Martha Larsen's mother.

Martha's parents, years before, had moved into a retirement community about ten miles east of Gainesville. Martha's mom, Flonnie, answered the phone and said, "Sure, come on out." It took us about two hours.

Martha's dad was a tall man, about 6′3″. Flonnie, on the other hand was 5′2″. I had never really gotten to know Martha's mom well, but I always thought of Napoleon when I was around her. In her house, she was the director and needed no assistant.

The blizzard persisted and dumped a couple of feet of snow on north Texas. We had to call the gallery in San Antonio and tell them we wouldn't be there. Needless to say, they weren't happy.

We passed the next few days warm and full of good food. We watched all the soaps on a very small TV, read everything in sight, and talked a lot. Martha's dad would sit in his big chair and doze. Sometimes he would participate in conversation and he would shake or nod his head when asked a question. Half the time he was right. He was deaf as a post.

Flonnie was a consummate card player. Bridge was her game. I had never played Bridge and at this time in her life, she was not inclined to put up with a novice. However, as boring as it is, I did know how to play Spades. As I recall, all you had to do was be able to count, and hold your mouth right.

She got the cards out.

The four of us sat around the table.

Let the games begin.

Wild Bill Hickok could not have shuffled with more precision. The cards flew across the table and the only thing missing on Flonnie was a green visor and a Derringer in her vest pocket. She had the look of a fox in her eye.

I sat across from Martha, so I played just before Flonnie, who was on my left. We played. As I would contemplate my next card and would pull it from my hand to lay down,

I noticed that, without looking at her hand, Flonnie would have already picked the card she would lay down after me. This went on for most of the afternoon. I don't think I was holding my mouth right.

Late in the afternoon, and probably because I was simply bored as hell, I reached out and put my left hand into the mouth of a rabid dog.

Almost in slow motion, and as Martha and her dad watched, I reached over with my left hand and touched the side of Flonnie's cards. I couldn't see the cards, but gently rubbed the corners where the numbers were as if I could tell what they were.

It was just a joke, damn it!

I looked over at Martha and could see the whites all around her eyes. Her mouth formed a big round "O." Her dad was just the same, except his left eye was twitching something fierce.

Flonnie didn't say anything. She slowly folded her cards together and gently laid them on the table in front of her. Quietly, she pushed her chair back, got up, and left the room.

Silence.

Nothing from Martha. Nothing from her dad.

We listened to the clock.

I wondered if this was what it was like for Wild Bill Hickok just before his brains were splattered over a hand of cards with a giant hole in the back of his skull from a .44 round, a short person standing there blowing smoke from the barrel of her Colt. A shiver ran down my back.

Suddenly, we were all aware of her presence as Flonnie came back into the room. She came back to her place at the table, sat, and quietly picked up her cards. "My play, I believe."

She looked at me and smiled the sweetest smile.

We played. I kept my hands to myself.

Aces 'N Eights.

Mike Larsen and Martha Schroeder were married on June 15, 1990 at Westminster Presbyterian Church in Oklahoma City. Back row, left to right, Dr. Mike Anderson, Ruth Larsen, Mike and Martha, and Carl and Flonnie Schroeder. Front row, from left, Martha's sons Jeffrey and Randall Fransen and Mike's daughter Kate.

THE VOICE

Where would we be if we didn't have that tiny, often irritating, voice back there in the undefined recesses of our minds? How many times have you started on an errand and that little voice says to you, "Might better go another way." Usually, you will not pay attention and sure enough, run into construction or snarled traffic and have to do a u-turn, retrace your tracks, and go another way.

Luckily though, that nagging little voice doesn't come from a "told you so" kind of guy. Usually. Sometimes it sits and listens. Sometimes it just sits. The question is, if you listen to that voice and make a change...were you right or not? No way to know.

There has been the occasion, however, when that little voice guides you along a perfect path. The right path. No question about it.

Thirty years ago, Martha and I started dating. Those were difficult times as we were both recovering from broken marriages. I had a daughter and Martha had two boys.

Martha Schroeder's two sons, Randall and Jeffrey Fransen.

Martha and Kate prior to the wedding.

It was a stroke of great fortune that I met Martha at the Oklahoma City Festival of the Arts and as wonderful as it was, I don't think either of us trusted our feelings.

I had not dated another artist since I was in college and, as I recall, back then art was the last thing on my mind when I was with a girl.

As time went by, Martha was doing shows on her own and I did shows and taught. Anything to make a buck. And we went to church. We went to the Presbyterian Church.

I was standing ten feet out in the ocean, water up to my chin, and the tide was coming in. I was a rabbit in a field full of smiling coyotes.

Martha and I were invited to a Christmas party by a woman at church. She was a small woman with busy hair and a booming voice. Couples only please.

After a fine dinner, pot luck, this small woman directed us all to gather in a circle.

Uh oh! The men were told to say something special about their partner, or at least say something interesting.

As it happened, Martha and I were the last couple in the circle. The man to my left would have to speak just before me. He looked as scared as I felt.

He and his wife had produced enough kids to populate a baseball team and people referred to him as..."unique."

Everyone had their turn as "wifely" compliments flew from the mouths of properly trained husbands.

Then it came the turn of the fellow next to me. It was quiet. He stared straight ahead and said, "I can touch my chin with my tongue." With that, he produced a pink rug that rolled out of his mouth, projected straight out and dropped, tickling his pointed chin. A man on the other side of the circle actually clapped.

He rolled it back in.

My turn. How can I match that?

There was a tickle at my primordial brain stem, my ancient self. A quiet voice said to me, a voice that I recognized but couldn't identify, "Don't screw this up."

I turned to my right and looked into Martha's face. I looked into those shining eyes behind huge red glasses, over a perfect field of freckles, and haphazard lips and asked, "Will you please marry me?"

Everyone clapped, even Mr. Unique who knew he had just been outdone.

I had listened to the voice.

Martha and Mike celebrate their marriage with the kids looking on.

Mike Larsen at the 1988 art show in Denver, Colorado.

MOT HOW

1988

Many years ago we were in a show in Denver, Colorado, and the whole thing went bad from beginning to end. First, we had to listen to an "authentic" Aztec band play the same tune over and over and over again and everyone's head was bursting. Second, sales were terrible and we had driven all the way from Oklahoma City.

When the show was finally over, it was late in the day and all we wanted to do was get the hell out of Denver. We were determined we were going to drive straight home even though it was 8:00 at night when we started.

Off we went, east on Interstate 70 for a couple of hours then south on 287, which was a two-lane. After two or three hours we easily decided that we needed to stop as soon as possible. Finally, we saw a town coming up ahead. As we got closer, we spotted a motel on the right. A neon sign blinked on and off. It said, "MOT HOW, MOT HOW, MOT HOW." We pulled into the parking lot of the Motel Howdy. We had to stop because there was probably nothing else for a thousand miles.

It was a small motel, maybe ten or twelve rooms. The whole thing was in a L-shape. Two cars were in the parking lot and a semi-truck hummed off in the distance. There was nothing else open that we could see on this side of a town that was very asleep. I drove up to the first door, which said "OFFICE," got out, and rang the bell where it said, "RING BELL." A light came on from inside and the porch light came on.

A little woman in a very large bathrobe answered the door and said, through the screen, "What?"

"Ma'am, we just wanted a room," I replied.

"Twenty dollars. No checks, no cards!"

I gave her the money and she gave me a key. There were no lights in the parking lot so I shined my headlights on the door until Martha could get inside. The place was so strange and the room smelled like cigarettes. And it was so dark.

Martha went to bed with her clothes on and I moved the only chair against the door and sat there with my Smith and Wesson .357 in my lap. The room was mostly quiet with the wall heater going on every now and then. I could tell Martha was not sleeping well at all.

I could also tell there was something going on outside our door. I peeked through the blind and saw several fuzzy, misty people wandering around our car. There was a small one on top of the car trying to pull out the antenna. I couldn't believe my eyes because some of them had arms that were way too long. And a couple of them didn't have arms at all.

As I held the blinds apart, they started looking at me. I caught my breath and heard a loud clunk. I had dropped the .357 and it was the "clunk" that woke me up from my dream. I was lucky the damned gun didn't blow my foot off.

I got up, went over and shook Martha, and said, "Let's get the hell out of here!" She got up, yanked her shoes on, held the gun as I opened the door, and watched as I threw all our stuff in the truck. We jumped in and pulled over to the highway. In my rearview mirror, I swear, I could see misty little people throwing rocks at us. We hit the highway and turned south into a small sleeping town. We got through the town pretty quick and started up a hill.

Just as we topped the hill, there it was.

I have always tried to remain a positive person because I know that we are all going to have bad times. We are all going to have bad shows. But staying focused and positive and continuing to work hard, I know that good things are just over the next hill. The problem has been, and is, that people, myself included, tend to pull up short, to stop too soon, to not look ahead because we are too busy looking at the ground.

Oh, woe is me. Wretched creature.

We drove through this bleak little town, up the hill, and there it was. Shining like that castle at Disneyland, the parking lot was full with, what I guessed to be, the people who had the good sense to go just a little further.

There it was, out there in the middle of nowhere . . . a Holiday Inn.

An old Packard dealership Mike and Martha Larsen found after leaving the Denver art show in 1988. It is not uncommon for them to stop during their travels and take pictures of things that peak their interest.

A picture of the original proposal piece for *Flight of Spirit* that burned in the January 5th studio fire.

Burn Baby, Burn

1991

Gather 'round the fire boys, and I'll tell you a tale.

On January 5, 1991, at 10:00 o'clock on a Saturday night my studio above The Jesus is Lord Pawn Shop burned in what was a magnificent fire. I would have paid to see it if it had been someone else's business being completely destroyed. Dozens of paintings, artifacts, and a fine library fueled the flames. My proposal painting for a huge project that was to become, possibly, a fixture at the Oklahoma State Capitol, also went up in smoke.

Martha and I had gone out that night for drinks and dinner. We had just returned home when we got the call from a friend who lived near the studio. I still to this day cannot remember how I felt as we drove down to the studio. Maybe it's just that I have blocked it out, or maybe the speed that I drove from our house to the studio did not allow thought.

We had to park a block away because the streets were blocked by the police and fire equipment. One officer stopped us from getting closer. I yelled at him, "That's my building!" He said calmly, "Well, what the hell you standing here for?" I ran up to the corner of the studio where, inside, my easel stood, with my finished proposal on it. Flames were roaring out the windows. I cursed and yelled at God. Someone took me by the arm and led me away. We had no insurance.

A fireman, who was rather round, took Martha and I half a block away to a shoe store that was serving as a command post. The round fireman turned out to be the chaplain for the fire department. He was very comforting and I don't believe I apologized to him for cursing so much.

He kept asking who our minister was. Martha spoke up and told him because the only words coming out of my mouth were words I still can't repeat. Fifteen minutes later as I was cursing at a reporter lady who wanted me to go on television, the most incredible thing happened. In walked a clown. Keep in mind, it was very cold outside. The clown was a very tall man wearing a huge fur cap with earflaps over a raincoat that must have belonged to his wife. All this was covering pajamas with Christmas tree designs and his feet stuffed in very fuzzy slippers. Our minister. Dear God. And to think, we had been listening to this man preach for years. The effect on me was that, at least I quit cursing at everything that moved. God works in mysterious ways I suppose. Our minister did stay with us until they knocked the fire down. I'll always remember him for that.

All my photographic records were lost. Dozens of paintings were lost. All my phone records and address files were lost. If it weren't for the fact that I could curse like a teamster, I might as well have been a newborn.

What got me through this without a doubt is the fact that Martha and I love each other very much and are able to talk our way through bad times. I highly recommend finding someone like that.

In the technology-age we live in now, when I finish a painting I immediately photograph it and send the photo to Martha's computer. Everything is backed up. All records are duplicated. Insurance is one of our big expenses. I would hate losing work to vandalism or a disaster like fire, but at least the financial ruin is checked. Every artist should do that.

10 Monday, January 7, 1991   THE DAILY OKLAHOMAN

— Staff Photo by Jim Beckel

A four-alarm fire Saturday destroyed the top floor of this building at NW 23 and Villa. Firefighters said the bottom floor, which housed a pawn shop, suffered smoke and water damage, but an apartment and studio above were destroyed.

4-Alarm Blaze Destroys Studio Of Indian Artist

By Brian Brus
Staff Writer

Indian artist Mike Larsen lost about $55,000 in uninsured art and supplies when a weekend fire raged through his studio.

The Saturday night fire blazed through a building at 2430 NW 23 that contained Larsen's studio, the A-1 Pawn Shop and an apartment. Oklahoma City fire department Maj. Jim Conner said the fire was started by an electrical short in the attic above the apartment.

"As far as my part's concerned, it's a total loss," Conner said. "The only thing I can be thankful for is that no one was hurt."

Larsen is a Chickasaw artist whose work has been featured on the cover of Oklahoma Today magazine and in the Kirkpatrick Center art museum. He also has won several awards as one of about 80 leading Indian artists from across the United States who participated in the Red Earth arts festival.

"The biggest loss was my library," Larsen said. "You spend 25 years collecting a large collection of books you use ... and suddenly it's gone."

Besides his art, Larsen said he lost Indian artifacts and pottery. Like much of his library, those cannot be replaced.

Native American artist Mike Larsen at work in this 1986 photo.

Larsen said his loss includes limited edition prints, posters and art supplies. He said nothing in the studio was insured.

Conner said damage to the structure was estimated at $66,000, and damage to contents, including Larsen's work, was $165,000.

The fire destroyed the upper level of the building. No injuries were reported.

The fire broke out about 8:40 p.m. Saturday, and quickly moved to four alarms as flames burst through the roof of the building's second story. The fire was extinguished about four hours later, Conner said.

Staff writer Melody Mills contributed to this report.

The fire that destroyed Mike Larsen's studio appeared in several newspapers throughout the Oklahoma City metro area.

With only a two-day extension to resubmit his proposal piece that burned in the fire, Mike Larsen was able to make the deadline and earn the commission for *Flight of Spirit*.

THE EFFECT

Through the good graces of the director of the State Arts Council, we were given extra time to complete another proposal for the large mural in the Oklahoma State Capitol building. We were competing with five other fine artists and were fortunate to eventually win the competition.

We quickly discovered that we had many more friends than we thought. One artist we knew showed up on our doorstep the morning after the fire with a check. Another artist organized an "art shower" for us and everyone showed up with money or art supplies, or both. Some of these people, I know, didn't have anything to spare but they left something for us.

This is the community of art.

We got through the aftermath of the fire rather quickly, partly because we had no choice. The proposal that burned was due two days after the fire. We were given two extra days to produce a new work so there was no time to wallow in pain and self-pity. We went out, bought supplies, set up a makeshift studio in our small kitchen, and went to work. I reproduced my proposal in the allotted time and we delivered the painting.

After we turned in our proposal there was still no time for remorse. We had to find another studio and I had to produce work. A really good friend and patron called and offered a building he owned to us that we could use as a studio for as long as needed. Rent free.

Again, the community of art.

I was busy working on a painting in this building a couple of months after the fire when I got a call from Betty Price, the director of the State Arts Council. The commission was mine.

I had won.

I hung up the phone with Betty, got up, walked over to my new easel, and the phone rang again. It was the editor of *Southwest Art Magazine*. I had the cover of the upcoming June issue. They had given me the cover of the June issue of *Southwest Art Magazine*.

We could have gone two different ways after the fire. Luckily, Martha and I are both very positive people, and very faithful. We knew the fire would set us back, but we weren't willing to let it defeat us. Defeat was not an option. Defeat should never be an option.

The fire that had blackened my past served only to illuminate my future. And strengthen my faith.

Mike Larsen's work graced the cover of the June, 1991 issue of *Southwest Art Magazine*.

The Larsen family at the warehouse with *Flight of Spirit* before it was delivered to the State Capitol. Note the small grey area on the back of the ballerina on the right. This was intentionally left blank to allow others to add a "brush stroke of their own" to the masterpiece.

THE BIG PICTURE

1991

In 1991, the year after Martha and I got married, The Jesus is Lord Studio burned. I was recovering from cancer surgery and radiation. Some kids in our neighborhood were playing with matches and sparked a grass fire, which nearly burned our house down. All I heard from our minister was, "Maybe you should start taking all this personally."

Thanks a lot. Just what I needed to hear.

It was indeed an interesting year. Luckily, I have a poor, and selective, memory so I only recall the good things.

In that year we were selected to paint the mural for the Oklahoma State Capitol. The mural would commemorate and honor the five ballerinas, all from Oklahoma, all Native American, and all world famous at the same moment in history. The mural was to go in the Capitol Rotunda on the fourth floor. It would be in the shape of a half circle, twenty-two feet along the base line and eleven feet high at the center.

The first thing to understand about painting an extremely large painting is mentally overcoming the size and not be intimidated. When I was going to the University of Houston, we had a really large German girl model for us in the nude. Now, that was intimidating. I digress.

I actually enjoy the possibilities of doing large murals and that has benefited us over the years. Some artists just cannot overcome the overwhelming power of a huge, empty canvas.

As we prepared for the mural, we rented a warehouse for six months. It was the only kind of structure that would accommodate a painting of such proportions.

The warehouse was one of many in a row of warehouses in northwest Oklahoma City. It was all metal. No air-conditioning.

It was spring when we rented the place. Spring quickly turned into summer. I had to go to work really early in the morning and quit early because of the heat that built up in the afternoon.

Developing a painting of great size has the same requirements as doing an easel painting. You sketch it on and work with the shadows and masses. You have to be very careful, however, with measurements. Exaggerations can be deadly on a large scale.

The painting progressed well and, as the commission was state funded, we had a lot of politicians come by for photo-ops. Every once in a while, prima ballerina Yvonne Chouteau would come by, always with a large bag of Fritos.

With the painting finished after roughly six months, you couldn't stir the place with a stick without hitting a politician, several of whom would smooth up beside me and whisper in my ear that it was they who were responsible for me getting the commission. Oh, please.

Mike Larsen atop the scaffolding during the installation of *Flight of Spirit*, more than forty feet above the ground floor of the Oklahoma State Capitol.

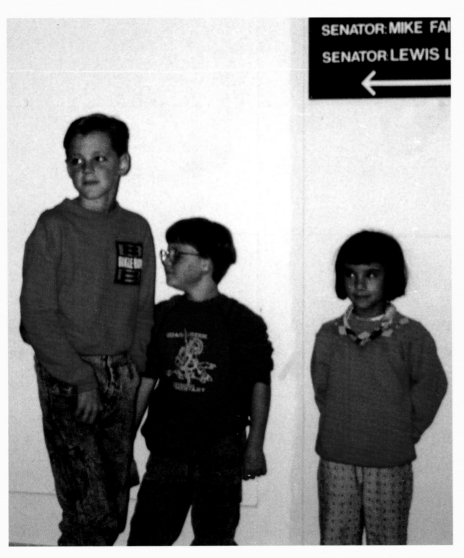

SENATOR: MIKE FAI

SENATOR: LEWIS L

Randall, Jeffrey, and Kate at the installation of *Flight of Spirit* at the Oklahoma State Capitol.

The canvas was taken down from the platform it had been attached to, rolled up like a tortilla, and delivered to the Capitol Building where it would be stretched on a wooden form and attached to the wall. There were lifts on either side of a constructed frame that would lift the painting up twenty feet so it could be installed. Because of the design of our Capitol Building, and the proximity of the scaffolding, a fall from that platform would have been more than forty feet.

Without thinking, I climbed up the scaffolding intending to help balance the painting as it went up. On top of the scaffolding were several sheets of plywood creating a kind of floor twenty feet up in the air. It wobbled from side to side. I looked over the side. I looked down. All I could think was, "Ohhhhhh shit." Martha was looking up. She had her hands to her cheeks.

I moved forward on the wobbly platform and as they started lifting the painting up, I heard a man actually yell the words, "Holy shit."

I looked towards the back of the platform. There was a young man there on all fours. He had on a bright red

Mike Larsen, second from left, with Oklahoma's prima ballerinas—Yvonne Chouteau Terekhov, Rosella Hightower, Maria Tallchief, Marjorie Tallchief, and Moscelyne Larkin—during the official dedication of *Flight of Spirit* at the Oklahoma State Capitol.

cowboy shirt with silver on the collars and fancy ostrich boots. A really nice camera dangled from his neck on a strap along with a silver bolo. He was an AP photographer and he was scared. He had made the mistake of looking behind him, over the back of the platform, over and down, into the abyss. He could see a drop of at least a mile.

He said, "Holy shit." again. I know that because I read his lips. There was no sound this time. I leaned over the edge and yelled, "People, we got a problem up here." It took quite a while for several men to get the youngster down. He was very proud and brave coming up, I'll give him that.

I don't remember if we even got AP photos that day or not and I have wondered what might have happened to that young man. I have an idea that Associated Press may have reassigned him to a desk, a desk he could hold on to lest he fall over the edge. With the painting in place, a big part of the adventure was over.

We all stood on the fourth floor landing and looked up at *Flight of Spirit*.

I noticed our oldest son, nearly twelve years old, leaning against the wall, looking up at the canvas. His little neck was stretched, his mouth open to a big "O." He was looking up at this painting that I had spent the last six months working on, sometimes seven days a week. A painting some were calling the "Jewel of the Capitol". God help me. I was very proud of it.

What's the old saying, "Pride cometh before a fall."

I asked him, "Well, what do you think?"

He looked at me as only a twelve-year-old boy can and said, "Dude, that's a big picture!"

Flight of Spirit was featured on the cover of the Winter 2003 issue of the Smithsonian's *National Museum of the American Indian* Magazine. Upon publication it was discovered that the image was printed reversed.

NATIONAL MUSEUM *of the*

American Indian

Winter 2003   Celebrating Native Traditions & Communities

En Pointe, Center Stage

The extraordinary story of Oklahoma's five legendary Native American ballerinas

Smithsonian
National Museum of the American Indian

BEAUTY IS IN THE EYE OF THE BEHOLDER

1987

Several years ago I was in an arts festival that I had participated in for many years. Some years were very good for sales, some years sucked really bad. It all seemed to average out over the years though.

The last year we were there was 1987. Toward the end of that week-long event, Martha and I were just waiting for the thing to be over so we could go home and kick back.

I had done a very large, and what I thought was a pretty good, painting for that show. We got some nice comments on it, but no sales. On the last day of the show, a lady came through and gave this particular painting a good looking over.

She came back by again.

And again.

Looking at that one painting.

From an early age, Kate would accompany her father and encourage visitors to his booth to "BUY ART."

I thought I had a sale for sure.

The fourth time she came by she came over to where we were sitting. I stood up and said "Hello."

She asked me, "Are you the artist?"

"Yes ma'am, I am."

She pointed at the painting and asked, "You painted that picture?"

Again I said, "Yes ma'am."

"That is, without a doubt, the ugliest thing I ever saw in my entire life!"

My brain was in a squeeze. My eyeballs were smoking. Before I could think I yelled at her, "Lady, get the hell out of my booth!"

She huffed and puffed then off she went.

I knew as sure as anything that the show officials would soon be running up and remove me from the show. But, no one came.

Just chalk it up as being the last straw.

But the show wasn't over yet.

One hour to go and I'm standing a short distance from my display. I looked up into a flawless blue sky and saw a seagull in the distance, coming straight toward me. Before I could react, he bombed me, like a German Messerschmitt, with a wad of white poop that hit me just above my shirt pocket and splattered all the way up to my left ear.

I went over and presented my avian gift to Martha and all we could do was howl. People looked at us like we were nuts.

Onward.

Two months later was the first ever Red Earth Indian Art Show. One of the works I had for this show was that very same "ugly" painting.

Wouldn't you know it? That painting won first place, Best of Show, Best of the Best.

Better yet. The judges who awarded me those prizes were Allan Houser and Dick West.

It keeps on coming.

That very same woman came to the Red Earth show and this time she brought a friend. I was standing close enough to hear her say to her friend, "See, didn't I tell you it was the ugliest painting ever?"

The comedy just never stops.

Mike Larsen in his studio with his Red Earth Best of Show *Search for the Mystery*.

The painting inspired by a bizarre incident in a Scottsdale, Arizona, Restoration Hardware hung in the Larsen home for two years.

Restoration Hardware

1995

Many years ago, Martha and I were in Scottsdale, Arizona, for a show. One afternoon we went shopping and happened into a Restoration Hardware store.

We were walking down the main aisle when off to my left I saw in my peripheral vision, a scene that couldn't have lasted more than a tenth of a second. An Indian man wearing a bright red stocking cap with flowing black hair was running toward the front door. He was wearing a World War II Army green great coat that rushed away behind him. I was astounded at what I was seeing and in that tenth of a second was thinking, "Where's my camera, where's my sketchbook?"

As that second proceeded, I slowly turned to my left to look at this scene that I knew I would be painting. As I turned my head to the left, the man with the red cap became a tall lamp with a bright red shade with long black fringe. The flowing Army green great coat became a long overstuffed couch.

It is difficult to describe the cartoon punch to my stomach. I did have the presence of mind to grab a price tag off a nearby coffee table and sketch down the idea on the back.

When we got home I expanded the idea, which became a very large painting. One of my best. I couldn't sell the painting for two years because Martha confiscated it to hang over our overstuffed couch. Which was of course, green.

One thing I try to tell young people when they ask about inspiration is to allow their mind's eye to constantly be aware. If you wait for that special moment or event, I can guarantee it won't come.

That painting I mentioned sold the first day Martha let me put it up for sale.

Men of Honor, by Mike Larsen, was displayed in the Pentagon rotunda. It was the only piece selected for an invitation-only display during Native American Month in November, 1990.

Memorial Day

2015

Several years ago, Martha and I took a road trip to the eastern states to visit Civil War battle sites. We had planned to visit twelve different sites. We went to two—Gettysburg and Antietam.

We came home after seeing just those two places because our hearts were so heavy. As we walked through those fields of battle, walked by thousands of markers of where men, young and old, had fallen, we were overwhelmed by the feeling of those men reaching up as we passed by, imploring us to remember, and to honor their memory.

Never forget, lest you lose this Republic!

We put out a new flag the next morning. I can't think of anything else to do. I'll call a couple of friends who served in Viet Nam. I don't know anyone personally who served in Iraq, but if we see a soldier we will thank them.

This Country, this Republic, is the most incredible success story in the history of the world.

Martha and I often talk about what those men gave up in life and fortune to write the Constitution and the Bill of Rights. The fact that George Washington should have been killed several times, but wasn't; that he was offered Kingship, but refused; that he crossed the Delaware virtually in front of the eyes of the British, simply makes me sit back and say...God placed his hand on this land and Blessed it.

Make no mistake though, should we forget...this Republic is lost.

A work inspired by and created to honor those in all branches of service.

Martha and Kate Larsen with *Oklahoma Indian Ballerina*, a tribute by sculptor Jay O'Meilia to Oklahoma's Indian ballerinas.

ROMAN

1991

He is well served who is well prepared.

When we were preparing to begin the ballerina mural back in 1991, we were fortunate because two of the ballerinas lived in Oklahoma. Yvonne Chouteau lived in Oklahoma City and Moscelyne Larkin lived in Tulsa.

We first made an appointment with Ms. Larkin, I believe on a weekend because she, at the time, was director of the Tulsa Ballet and her weekdays were packed. We drove over to Tulsa for our interview with her and took our daughter, age five, with us.

We arrived at her house and she met us at the door. She was a lovely woman in her seventies. She took us into their den and introduced us to her husband who was in failing health. He was in his pajamas and a robe. It was mid-afternoon. He was seated in a large, overstuffed recliner, which was in front of a very large television.

He was very gracious and offered to entertain our daughter while Martha and I interviewed Moscelyne in the living room. The three of us went into the living room and we talked with this great woman for over an hour. I kept noticing a soft buzzing sound and put it off as air-conditioning.

She recounted many, many stories of her performances from New York to Moscow and the wonderful people she had worked with. I kept noticing that buzzing sound.

Opportunity knocks softly.

We finished our interview and the three of us walked back into the den. Leaning all the way back in the overstuffed recliner, was Moscelyne's husband. He was sound asleep, quietly snoring. That was the buzzing I had been hearing.

Our daughter was folded into his arms, sound asleep. Folded into the arms of this, one of our greatest all-time ballet dancers, Roman Jasinski. They had both been watching cartoons on the television. They had been watching Bugs Bunny. Together.

I didn't have my camera.

Little Round Top, completed by Mike Larsen on site in May, 2012 during his and Martha's trip to visit the Civil War battlefields.

Shadows Rushing By

2012

"Well hell boys, that ain't nothing," referring to the view of Little Round Top from a mile to the south on July 3, 1863.

"We took this ground yesterday. It ain't very good ground, but it's ours, for a bit.

"Having won the day yesterday, Lee meant to take the advantage and charge, against the advice of his Generals.

"We all did what we was told and off we went, across open ground for a mile or so before there was any cover. Fire from hell was coming at us from three sides. Men and boys were falling faster than you could count.

"There was a small mountain a few hundred yards ahead and we meant to take it. It was called, Little Round Top.

"We ran over small hills and a creek, the smell of burnt powder so thick you couldn't breathe. The burns on my face from my own rifle hurt like hell.

"We finally got close enough to the mountain that we could look up. It was a small mountain, more like a hill. Problem was, the rocks, big ones, as far as you could see. Scattered all over. We were going to have to go over the damned things. I know they gave us some small cover but shit fire.

"Fire was coming down on us from the top. I never saw the men up there, all I saw was fire. I stopped at a really big rock to rest a sec and looked back to where we started. I could see him. I could see him back at the tree line. The Man. The Man himself, astride a magnificent horse.

"I turned around and reloaded and climbed over the rock. Looked like we might be halfway up. I could make out men in blue. We charged up, yelling and shooting.

"Then. The shooting slowed, and I seen them. They were charging us, down from the top, bayonets out front.

"A tall man, with long mustaches was leading them, leading the 20th Maine. General Joshua Lawrence Chamberlain was leading them. His saber in his right hand. He and I came so close I could smell his breath. I placed a cap and raised my rifle. No time to fire.

"I didn't feel anything but great pressure. I couldn't pull a breath.

"I looked down and all I could see was the tall man's hand and the hilt of his saber. He grabbed my shoulder with his left hand and pulled the saber from my body with his right. The entire blade was bright red. I don't remember falling, but I guess I did. I do remember looking up at the purest, blue sky, the smell of sweet grass in my nose, as shadows kept rushing by. "

Shadows rushing by.

Shadows rushing by.

We have a really good friend who is a fine author, historian, and an avid runner. A twenty-mile run is a piece of cake for him. Myself, I try to avoid running at all costs. Anyway, a passion of his is the Civil War period and he was determined a few years ago to make the run, like those brave men did back in 1863, up Little Round Top. He made the trip, and the arrangements, and made it happen.

On the appointed day, he got up early, started where the tree line would have been, and ran. He ran slowly, toward the small mountain about a mile away. When he got to Round Top he started up, his only baggage, a plastic bottle of water.

He immediately encountered boulders and large rocks. There was no running now, only climbing and hopping, and falling. He continued, climbing, stepping over, jumping, until he was about two-thirds the way to the summit, then, "No more!" was all he could think. He looked up at the thirty or more yards he still had to go. He leaned against a large stone watching people shoot at him, not with Springfields or Sharps, but with Nikons and Kodaks.

He looked all the way back to where he had started thinking he might see the man on the big white horse, but there was no way. He looked down the hill he had just climbed with such a feeling of loss and emptiness, he cried. A cold breeze moved over him but it was of no comfort. It was a shadow passing by.

Mike Larsen painting at the base of Little Round Top.

Martha and I love road trips. We try and take one every year. Several years ago, we decided our next trip would be a visit to the great battlefields of the Civil War. We mapped out about a dozen sites and off we went. We went through Ohio for a necessary stop with relatives, and then drove straight to our first, of twelve, stops. Gettysburg.

We saw the sites, bought some souvenirs, and ate some really good food. The next morning we drove to the top of Little Round Top. We spent half that day looking down the hill, at what those men did, at the effort, the death. The horror.

We didn't talk much that evening.

The next day, we drove down to Antietam and spent the day there. We did the tour. We saw where so many thousands had died. We walked the trails, we saw the markers. The markers were everywhere. As we would walk by these markers, I would wonder if these boys lying there would notice our shadows rushing by.

When we drove to the hotel that afternoon, Martha looked over at me and said, "I've seen all I can. Let's go home."

One of Mike Larsen's completed still life works following a demonstration in his studo.

Paper Towels

MID 1980's

Back in the late 1970's and early 1980's I taught a weekly art class to anyone who wanted to come. No qualifications. No requirements. Except money, of course. I did accept checks.

In those years, I believe I might have had three, maybe four students with talent. One student in particular had enough talent that he could have made a mark in the art world, but as it happened, he was unwilling to make the leap.

I fully understand. It would be really hard to give up the security of a stable job, a weekly paycheck, paid insurance, and paid vacation. Jeepers, maybe I'll try and find something like that.

One thing I always did during the course of those classes was to do a monthly demonstration.

Over the years, Martha and I have attended demonstrations by good artists, given the opportunity. I would never take classes from these people but I love to watch them work. One thing I always noticed during these demonstrations was the way the artists worked their audiences. They entertained.

One painter actually sang. Good thing for him he made his living as a painter.

Occasionally, one group or other will ask me to do a demonstration and I usually agree. Seven or eight years ago I did a demonstration at a museum in which I happened to have work. The lighting was bad. I had no room to move around. I had to stand on plastic sheeting, which crackled with every move I made, but it was a museum, after all. Declining their request would not have been smart, and I try to be smart.

One thing about doing a demonstration is you have to try to keep your mind clear. Thinking just gets in the way. Too much preparation can actually stifle creativity. Doing a demonstration in front of a crowd that will include people who might be buying your work is like being on stage, in a one-act play. You are the only actor. You have to get your lines right. There are no second chances. Do or die.

The thing is, God help me, I love it.

One of the secrets of having a good demo is having a well-placed "friendly" face in the audience. I will always try and put Martha front and center so when I look back to explain something, I can look directly at her and, if she is not picking her nose or making a face, I won't have to engage anyone else.

Because I paint in acrylics, I usually don't put my paints out until the last minute. My easel will be up and ready. I will situate the model or adjust the still life. I will move the lights so that they create as much shadow as possible.

Breathe in breathe out.

I will put out my paints, and two, maybe three brushes. The audience is usually quiet at this point.

Begin.

Understand that beginning a painting is much like conducting an orchestra. You raise your hands. You roll back on the heel of your off foot for balance. You lower your brush. And start.

I stand as far away from the canvas as I can and still be able to touch it with the business end of the brush. I'll lean forward as I visually find the center of the canvas and delicately place a small spot of paint there. Then I'll back away, turn toward the audience and ask, "Any questions?"

This usually gets a laugh and relaxes them, and me.

There is, however, real purpose to putting that mark in the center of the canvas. As I design the elements of the painting, whether it be a model or still life, with linear strokes of my brush, I will place the subject on the canvas always keeping an eye on that center mark, and staying away from it. When the painting is as finished as I want it, I'll paint over that very first mark.

The painting will proceed quickly as I mass in areas of hair or shadow and begin placing color and light, pushing color into the background. This is a very exciting time and to maintain control of myself, and the painting, I will stop after about twenty or twenty-five minutes and invite questions. The questions are usually good, involving things like why I chose a particular color or why did I use my finger instead of a brush to mix skin color.

During one demonstration, there was an obvious student there, franticly taking notes, and a woman...a very pale woman, with flaming red hair, mouth open as she held her right hand to her chest. I hoped she wasn't having a heart attack.

Questions had stopped, I returned to my canvas. After another fifteen or twenty minutes, the painting sparkled and I signed it. I turned toward the audience and absently started cleaning my brush with a paper towel. Hands went up. The student stopped writing. The questions were interesting. I enjoy this part.

The little crowd finally had their fill and I was just about to invite them up for a closer look at the painting when a hand went up. The pale woman with the flaming hair had her hand up. Her mouth was still wide open as she put both hands to her chest.

I was ready to explain to her in deep detail whatever it was she needed to better understand about what I had just spent the last hour doing.

I was ready.

Everyone else was ready.

She brought forth her right hand as though she were brushing aside the very air between us and asked, "What brand of paper towels do you use?"

Mike Larsen's first demonstration as part of the Holiday Small Works Show at the Gilcrease Museum in Tulsa was in November, 2007, during Oklahoma's Centennial.

Black Leggings by Mike Larsen.

HONOR

2000

A very long time ago, The Kiowa people left the area around the Yellowstone in a quest to find a new home. They packed up home and hearth and headed south. They passed through the lands of the Arikara, Crow, Cheyenne, and any number of smaller tribes finally coming to what is now Oklahoma. As this large number of Kiowa people continued south in Oklahoma, it began to rain. It rained for days and days and seemed as if it would never stop.

After weeks of continual rain they decided to just stop. They ended their journey in southcentral Oklahoma and made camp.

In the rain.

They could not make fires because there was no dry wood.

They made camp, sat in their lodges, and prayed. As morning came, their prayers were answered. The rain stopped. The sky cleared.

They stepped out of their lodges into a clear day and found that they had stopped and made camp at the bottom of a small mountain. They prayed and sang and named the small mountain "Rainy Mountain." This became the home of the Kiowa people, and remains home to this day.

Most of my paintings come after an encounter with history, sometimes brief, sometimes not. My relationship with Rainy Mountain came about because of a commission to do eight murals for a resort here in Oklahoma. Four of the murals were to deal with the history of the Kiowa people about whom I knew little.

Coming Out of the Yellowstone by Mike Larsen.

INTRODUCTION TO RAINY MOUNTAIN

A great spokesperson for the Kiowa is N. Scott Momaday who wrote a book about the mountain. This was a perfect place to start so I drove out to Santa Fe, New Mexico, to interview and photograph him. We talked at length about Kiowa history and he suggested I visit the mountain. He gave me the names of a very old Kiowa couple in Oklahoma who would take me to the mountain and introduce me. I felt as though I was being thrown back into history.

I came back home and made arrangements to visit these two old people who lived at the foot of Rainy Mountain. Very traditional and very necessary.

I drove to their home. They invited me inside and as protocol dictated, we visited for most of the morning. No mention of why I had come. I ate way too much of some kind of meat, several sweets, and gallons of coffee. I looked at every family photo in the house.

Finally, the old man stood, put on his black hat and said, "Rainy Mountain is waiting for you, young man."

We drove over to the mountain. Rainy Mountain is very unimpressive. He and I got out of the car.

"Well, there she is. And she enjoys quiet."

With that he got back into the car.

I took my camera and walked toward the famous mountain shooting film of a completely unimpressive scene. It would have been rude not to take lots of photos.

I was forty or fifty yards out in very tall grass when the old man hollered out his window, "You might keep an eye out, the rattle snakes are pretty bad this year."

Thanks a lot.

I went away from there that day unimpressed with the mountain, but overwhelmed with the history.

The painting, measuring eight feet by ten feet, turned out well, not because of what I saw but because I was able to understand what this place means to these people. Understanding is the key.

When I got back in the car that day, the old man looked at me and quietly said, "I have lived my entire life in the shadow of that mountain. Do you understand?"

"Yes sir, I do."

We talked for a while longer over coffee and pie, and the old man told me of his fear that their history was fading fast because their young people were leaving the land, having put away the past.

As an artist who relies heavily on history, I feel blessed to be able to portray these places and events that will, in a way, last for generations.

Researching the history keeps me honest and allows me to honor the people who lived out their lives in the shadow of their history helping build this country— this Oklahoma.

The Society of Twelve Warriors by Mike Larsen.

WHEN HISTORY LIVES

It was a smoky, dusty day. And hot. The wind was harsh and smelled nasty. Maybe because of that mountain in the far away that was being loud and puffy. The man continued working. He was a short man, hairy and stout. He was cutting up the animal he had killed with a sharp stone. His hands were bloody. He reached over and made a smear on the flat rock next to where he was working. He glanced at the smear with hooded eyes and quickly drew back from the rock because he thought the smear looked like the animal he was butchering.

The image scared him but at the same time thrilled him. He reached over and touched the red animal on the rock. Then he stuck his hand into the belly of the small beast on the ground. He pulled out two fingers covered with new blood and again touched the image. Moving his fingers, he delicately pushed the blood around and found that the animal looked even more real. He ran to get the others to show them this dream animal that lived on a rock.

This was forty-thousand years ago.

There have been times when something will happen with a painting that both scares and thrills and I'll call Martha and say, "Martha, come quick, you've got to see this." Maybe the only difference between me and that man forty-thousand years ago is that I'm not short and hairy.

Throughout our time on this Earth, art has been our connection with the past. It is so connected with history, it makes history live. That man, all those years ago, did not show off that smear to document the killing of an animal. He did not know he was being creative. What he saw was magic. He saw a spirit that he couldn't identify. He saw power. He may have produced other smears that were even better. Maybe not. Others may have been motivated to try their hand at "painting." Maybe not.

The Code Talkers by Mike Larsen.

Chief Joseph by Mike Larsen.

As time progressed, thousands of men who had a gift left their drawings and paintings on the walls of countless caves across Europe, Africa, and Asia. It was surely magic and an effort to secure power over the beasts they hunted, not to document anything.

It is impossible to say when painting may have developed into what we might consider the Modern Era; but it was, and is, a continual progression. The constant is the involvement with history in art over the ages.

I hated Art History in college and my grades reflected that. I wish now that I had paid more attention in class. When I do paintings now, history is always my first or second consideration. More often than not, I will read an item of history and it will quickly become a visual, then a process, then a fact. In this context I find art much like math, which, as it happens, was the only thing in school I was good at.

Albert Einstein was an artist. I wish I could better understand the man, how he envisioned, how he processed, and how he came to the conclusions he did.

God is an artist. He envisioned, processed, and the conclusion cannot even be imagined it is so fantastic.

Art is what keeps history from being forgotten. Maybe that is one of the purposes of art. As an example, when I look at paintings of the Civil War by Winslow Homer, I am first struck by the power of the painting, but gradually look past the wonderful color and brushwork into what he was portraying. The history then reaches out and pulls me in. When I study the history of this great country, I will always go to the paintings first.

The development of our great national parks came about because of art. The paintings about Meriwether Lewis and William Clark or the incredible portraits by George Catlin entice us to study our history. The history of our country, the history of the astounding Indian nations that lived here long before the "Cloud People" were first seen, continue to fill our imaginations through Art.

The history of the wars, here and across the globe, the history of our adventures in space, the history of art itself, all could be portrayed in a hundred-thousand volumes that didn't contain a single written word. I could go on and on, but I don't want to be redundant, repeat myself, or say the same thing over and over again.

So!

Tecumseh by Mike Larsen.

Jeffrey and Mike planting a plum tree in the front yard of the family home
for Martha on Mother's Day, 1995.

The Plum Tree

In 1993 Martha and I bought our first house in Oklahoma City. It was a beautiful two-story Spanish style and we bought it from our preacher—the one who came to us the night of The Jesus is Lord Pawn Shop fire.

The house was on Saintsbury Court in the Lansbrook addition. Martha spent a lot of time in the front garden for it needed a lot of work. We had lived there for two years when, on Mother's Day, I stopped at Horn's Nursery at the Classen Circle and bought a small tree for the front yard.

When I got home, I got out the tools, looked up, and there was our younger son Jeff. He wanted to help me dig the hole. We placed the tree and stood back for a look. It was a fine tree for sure, about five feet tall with beautiful purple leaves. It was a plum tree and its trunk was about as thick as my thumb.

The house was a good place for us to grow as a family and we needed it. Martha had two boys and I had a daughter. I think the house needed us too. The kids quickly made friends and it was interesting and edifying how many of those friends showed up at our dinner table. Martha was a very good cook. The word got around. Many evenings around six, two or three would just happen by, "oh, you mean dinner's ready?"

Martha always had more food prepared than just for us, just because. We have followed the lives of those youngsters. Some went on to do great things, some we lost track of. I have a feeling though that Martha's apple pie accounted for several of those success stories, and I also have a feeling that those young people would agree. Martha was able to feed them more than pie, she fed them family.

Before I knew it, when I'd come home from the studio and look at that plum tree, it was taller than me.

During those years on Saintsbury, we were involved with many art projects. We did a series of paintings called "Shamans of the Nations". Another series was called "Great American Indian Leaders". We painted eight murals for the Oklahoma Arts Institute at Quartz Mountain State Lodge. Four of the paintings were on the history of the Kiowa people and four on the history of the Institute.

While doing one of those murals, I had a fall at the Paseo Studio and broke my hip. While at the Mercy Hospital ER, I was carted into the x-ray room. The technician there was a lovely young woman with very large breasts. While she helped me onto the x-ray table, pain shot up my leg and hip as though I'd been shot. I grabbed for the closest thing at hand—two 40D beauties. I apologized profusely. She just smiled at me and said, "That's okay, honey. I get that a lot."

I recovered on Saintsbury and after a couple of months Martha drove me to the studio to work. The plum tree was at least seven feet tall now and very full. A mockingbird was nesting in the tree squawking at us. When I finished the Quartz Mountain murals, I was working on crutches.

One thing that appealed to our kids as they grew older and finished high school was the fact that our house had a beautiful, open, winding staircase. They all wanted to have their prom pictures taken on the stairs. So did their friends.

We lived through many adventures in the Saintsbury house. Our younger son, Jeff, tripped over a leaf, fell, and broke his collarbone. Our daughter, Kate, fell down by the lake and busted her chin open. Our oldest, Randall, who is quite tall, learned the value of helmets when he did a double flip on his roller blades. A herd of geese at the lake chased my mother, who was 85 at the time. The lead goose made her jump with a nasty bite on her backside. I didn't think Mother could jump that high.

On a hot summer afternoon as Martha and I were walking home from the lake, as we approached the house, Martha commented, "Look how tall the plum tree is." It was about nine feet tall. It became apparent, and quickly, that soon we were going to be in this grand house with no children. They were all going to be in college. We started thinking about looking at land somewhere, something we had longed for forever.

We had spent time in Cody, Wyoming, a lovely place, except in the mud months. We thought about Taos, New Mexico, where real artists live, but there was no zoning and nice houses were standing right next to, hmmm, dumps. We looked at the Wet Mountain Valley in Colorado. Astoundingly beautiful. But, it was when we were driving home from Colorado that we looked at one another and came to our senses—we are Okies. When we got home we called realtors all around Payne County to keep an eye out for a small, perfect, piece of land.

The realtor in Perkins called. "We have a square forty. It's nearly perfect, just east of town." On our way to look at that land, as we pulled out of our drive, we paused to look at the plum tree. It was taller still. We listened to the mockingbirds chattering in their nests.

We drove to Perkins and they took us out to the land. It was crowded with cows and had several ruined trailer houses on it. But, it was perfect. We decided to call it La Fortuna.

We drove back to Saintsbury Court and sat for quite a while in the driveway looking at a beautiful plum tree. That tree had grown so much. It had become a living symbol of our life in this house. We left Saintsbury Court in 2003 to spend our lives on a beautiful piece of land east of Perkins, Oklahoma. Yet that home on Saintsbury Court we will not forget.

Sometimes when we go to Oklahoma City we drive out to visit the Saintsbury house. The plum tree is ever bigger and grander. It waves as we pass by. We wave back.

Jeffrey and Mike eight years later in front of the plum tree they had planted together in 1995.

A painting by Mike Larsen depicting the land in Perkins where he and Martha built their forever home and a studio.

THE GIFT

DECEMBER 31, 1897

It's an anxious affair coming into a new town. You don't know the lay of the land. You don't know the people. You don't know the politics or which way the wind blows.

U. S. Marshal Bill Tilghman rode into Perkins, Oklahoma from the south and pulled up on the east side of Main Street in front of Ray Utter's East Side Saloon. He sat in the saddle for a short while then dismounted. The grey sighed. Bill was a big man. He walked into the saloon and surveyed the place well. There were a few men at the great wooden bar and some at the few tables, drinking with girls in bright dresses. There was a stairway, which led up to where the girls conducted business and a door to the back. He walked over to the bar, dropped four bits, and said to the barkeep, "Rye."

As his drink was coming, the marshal kept an eye out the front window. Directly across the street was the town marshal's office. Two men were sitting in chairs just outside the office door. The one on the right was too big for his clothes and had a star pinned to his shirt.

Bill threw back his drink and walked out the saloon door. He walked over to the grey horse and, taking the reins from the rail, positioned the animal between himself and the jail across the street. He reached down, flipped the loop off the hammer of his Scofield, and pulled it out of the well-oiled holster. He thumbed the barrel forward and dropped a sixth round into the chamber and closed the weapon with a snap. He replaced the pistol.

Taking the reins with his left hand, he walked the horse across the street and tied him in front of the jail. The two men had been watching him but kept their seats. Bill stepped onto the porch and quietly said to the town marshal, "You have a prisoner in your jail by the name of Maydele. I'm taking him over to Guthrie for trial. I want him out here. I want him out here now."

The Perkins town marshal smirked, looked up at the big man, and said, "I got your man but he's going to trial here in Perkins not in by God Guthrie."

It takes about half a second to blink your eyes but in less than half that amount of time Bill Tilghman pulled the heavy Scofield .44 and jammed the barrel against the cheek of the marshal. It was fully cocked. The Perkins town marshal said, "I'll go get him."

Tilghman replied, "I'll wait right here." A few minutes went by. The prisoner came out the door. Alone.

Tilghman took the man and his big grey horse and they walked up the street to the livery, on their way to Guthrie.

Mike and Martha Larsen built their home on 40 acres east of Perkins in 2004.

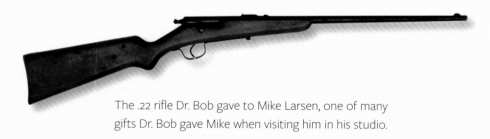

The .22 rifle Dr. Bob gave to Mike Larsen, one of many
gifts Dr. Bob gave Mike when visiting him in his studio.

MOVING ON INTO THE 20TH CENTURY

Mother married when she was fourteen, my dad was thirty-
five. The year was 1931. They lived in Oklahoma City and
with both of them working, made about twenty-eight dollars
a week. For Dad's birthday in 1932, Mother bought him a
new bolt action, single shot, .22 rifle from Sears-Roebuck
for $3.75. Many years later, Dad gave the rifle to my older
brother. Years later still, my brother gave the rifle to his son
who, after waiting about a week, sold it. The rifle was never
offered to me.

In 2004, Martha and I bought land just east of Perkins,
Oklahoma. The realtor we used was located on Main Street
in Perkins. I told the realtor that I would be needing studio
space if he heard of anything. He said, "I got just what you
need." He walked us down to the southeast side of our one-
block long Main Street and we three stood in front of what
once was Ray Utter's East Side Saloon.

We went in.

I had come from "The Jesus is Lord Pawn Shop Studio" to
the "Ray Utter Saloon Studio." Ah, the irony of it all.

The two-story stone building had two very large rooms on
the bottom floor. The front room is where the bar had been. It
showed no ill effects from the bullet holes in the walls or from
the bear that lived in the saloon in 1903. Sometime during that
year, the bear had torn the place to pieces after it saw its own
reflection in the giant mirror above the bar. Because all the
shooters were drunk at the time, there are differing accounts

of how many shots were fired before the bear died.

There was an angular indention on the south wall from the stairs to the second floor brothel. We fixed the place up and I went to work.

One day a little man came into the studio. His wife was with him. She was a very small woman with sparse white hair and bright blue eyes. He was a retired doctor. For forty or more years, this place had been his office. I was delighted.

Dr. Bob came in often in the following months. He always had his wife with him and he always brought me a present. Sometimes it would be a silly hat or an old *Playboy* Magazine, but he always brought something.

One day he came in and had a long package under one thin arm. He walked over to me and said, "This damned thing has been leaning behind my door for at least thirty years. I saw it the other day and for some reason, thought of you."

I unwrapped the package. It was an old rifle. I pulled back the bolt. It was a single shot .22.

He looked at me and said, "I bought that rifle back in 1932. Got it at Sears-Roebuck for $3.75. For some reason, thought you might like to have it."

That rifle hangs on a wall of my Studio. I look at it several times a day.

Dr. Bob did give me a gift that day, but it wasn't that old rifle. The gift he gave me was a memory. A memory of a young girl, all those years ago. A memory of my mother.

Mike and Martha Larsen in front of their studio on Main Street in Perkins. The studio was located in the old Ray Utter East Side Saloon.

The Arrival by Mike Larsen is installed at the Chickasaw Cultural Center in Sulphur, Oklahoma.

The Arrival

2010

1000 A.D. or so, somewhere in the deep Southwest.

The maize this season rose barely above the topsoil. I cannot remember the last time I had enough water to drink or to wash my body. My babies all died along with most of the old people. I sit and watch them as they just dry up and die.

The Elders have watched and seen. They have had many talks with the Holy Men and it was finally decided—they must leave this place.

They gathered all the people together. The Holy Men constructed a tall pole with Holy things on top. The oldest and most Holy one said simply, "We are leaving this place and will travel in the direction we are shown by this pole." We will start in the direction of the rising sun." That's what we did.

"Go East young man."

All of us, men, women, and children gathered all our possessions and as dawn came we followed the Elders toward the new sun.

At the end of each day, the Holy Men would plant the Magic Pole in the ground, pointing straight up. As the sun rose the next morning, the pole would miraculously be leaning in the direction we were to travel that day. It always pointed to the east.

Generations passed and new Elders replaced the old. We stopped each season to plant and sow then moved on. We had babies and buried our dead along the way. Storytellers kept our children informed as to why we were always traveling.

We met many different peoples along the way and affected their lives with our traditions as they also affected us with theirs. We stopped in several places along the way for extended periods and left evidence of our being.

After many generations and after leaving countless of our people in the ground, we came to the largest river anyone had ever seen. With much effort, we crossed it.

On the most important dawn in our history, the Magic Pole remained erect, pointing straight up into a clear blue sky. We all made plans, built lodges, said prayers, and began planning our lives again.

At that time, our leaders were two brothers, Chicksa and Chocta. They were equal in power and presence.

One morning the Magic Pole was leaning. Just a little. But leaning.

Chocta argued with his brother that the people should keep moving. Chicksa said "no." Chocta took half the people and left. Chicksa stayed. We became two peoples. Both these groups became great warrior nations in the eastern woodlands, dominating many other tribes in the area. Peace through strength lasted for many, many years.

The calm was deceiving.

In 1541 the Chickasaw people came face to face with the devil. Hernando DeSoto and many soldiers came up from Florida into the land of the Chickasaw.

Warriors reported to the Elders about creatures in shiny clothes and hairy faces that really smelled bad. They had with them many, many small round animals that made a grunting sound. The most astounding though, was the magnificent animals they rode upon—a creature so graceful and regal with fine lines and a beautiful head.

The Elders and Holy Men gathered the people and together they greeted these creatures with gifts of food and jewelry. The people were astounded by the smell of the newcomers. The leader of these "men" dismounted. He was a short man, arrogant and loud. He did not offer gifts.

The time spent with these Spaniards was a bad time for the Chickasaw people. The Spaniards never gave, they only took. After a period of time in which the Spanish demanded, offended, and punished the people, a secret decision was made among the Elders, to take no more.

The Spanish were driven from the land of the Chickasaw. Many were killed or wounded. The Spaniards left on the run, leaving behind many of the round, grunting animals, many weapons and...horses...lots of horses.

Over the years that followed, the Chickasaw men developed a unique relationship with the horse. They became experts at breeding and over many generations developed what became known as the Chickasaw Horse, a horse short and quick, extra strong in the rear, excellent for a warrior in the woodlands. Many generations forward, the blood of that animal flows through the American Quarter Horse.

After dealing with the Spanish, the people thought they had seen it all with foreign people. However, they had yet to meet the French, or the English.

They had no comprehension of the Americans.

Understanding politics among Indian people is reasonably simple; two parties would go at one another. If the party of the first part was stronger than the party of the second part, people would die, and the party of the first part would take everything they could carry and go home. If each party were equal in strength, then compromise would be in order. Each side would accept some responsibility and go home and honorably do what was decided, if in fact, anyone could remember what the argument was about in the first place. Usually everyone would just forget the whole thing.

The Americans were different. They said they would drive the Indians from the eastern woodlands, and that's exactly what they did. They were driven to a place called, "the Indian Territory."

GO WEST YOUNG MAN.
The Choctaws were shooed away first into Indian Territory, the Chickasaws went later. After spending a lot of money, the Chickasaws were allowed a portion of Choctaw land. The Choctaws decided that the Chickasaws could have the western part of their land. How magnanimous. The story goes, that this grand gesture would assure the Chickasaws would be a fine buffer between the Choctaw and the fierce Kiowa-Apache to the west. Gift horses sometimes have false teeth, don't ya' know.

In 1837, the Chickasaw people arrived by train at Boggy Depot, Oklahoma, and set about, on foot, to their final destination. After many miles and much hardship, and many deaths, the people finally arrived at what was to become a true homeland for the Chickasaw people.

As long as rivers flow and winds blow.

Mike Larsen used his daughter and grandson as models for the young mother and child in *The Arrival*, permanently installed at the Chickasaw Cultural Center in Sulphur, Oklahoma.

In 2010, we were commissioned to do a monumental sculpture depicting the arrival of the Chickasaw people at their Oklahoma homeland. The work is nine feet tall and includes nine people, all Chickasaw models.

The models included a Lighthorse policeman, a legislator, our daughter, and a young full-blood man who I became good friends with. This young man modeled for me many times for other works and he told me much about his history and life. But like every Indian man who ever lived, there were some things he kept.

One of the models was an old woman, Pauline Walker. She was a cornerstone of the sculpture piece and stood right in front of the young full-blood man. The work depicts an extended family unit as they have just topped a rise and are looking upon their new homeland. They are all looking forward except for a young woman holding an infant, our daughter and grandson, She is looking back to where they came from, not out of remorse, but out of remembrance.

If we are to move forward in life, we must not forget our past and all the past has to teach us.

The big day of the dedication came. All the models were there except one...Pauline. She was ninety-five-years old and very ill. Her time was coming soon and we all knew it. There was no way she could be there. You could feel the emptiness at her absence.

A lot of people. A lot of speeches. I had to wear a suit and give a speech, gag me. Speeches over, we all went up to where the sculpture was. It was unveiled. Very exciting. Lots of photos and handwork and gradually the crowd drifted away.

I wondered off and after a while came back to visit with the bronze.

The young, full-blood Chickasaw man was there. He was dressed in a beautiful dark ribbon shirt and his black hair shone in the sun. He was standing in front of the old woman, his hands raised caressing her bronze face. He smoothed back her bronze hair. There was sadness in his eyes. He noticed me and quickly dropped his hands. We stood there in an awkward silence, and then I asked, "Do you know her?" He took her bronze hand in his, like a child, and said, "She is my grandmother."

I go to the Chickasaw Cultural Center when I can and I always go up to visit the bronze. The hands of Pauline are shiny from the rubs of many of the people. I will have visited with our bronze daughter and grandson, and leave happy. I will also leave, untouched, the newly-cut flowers spread out at the old woman's feet.

Ann Sherman . . . Meira

isn't she wonderful

I have a friend. Her name is Meira, which means, "One who gives light."

It is a fitting name for this woman because she is a professional photographer, a really good one.

Meira and I have known each other for many, many years. She photographs my work several times a year. She is a solid woman, not fat by any means, but solid. Strong as an ox, she is a person you could trust to watch your back in any situation.

She has crazy hair, not naturally black I think, but sometimes it might be bright red or even green. Her daughter is an aspiring hair stylist and Meira is a willing experimental dummy. She is one of my best friends. Meira is Jewish.

She and I often talk at length and the conversations sometimes lead to her Jewish heritage. This is always fine with me because Martha and I have always had lengthy conversations about the Hebrew experience as we watch the nightly news and the continual attempt to destroy the very idea of Judaism.

As a rabid student of history, I look at the incredible contribution of the Jewish people for thousands of years and just sit in awe and thanks. I have told Meira of my thoughts, and even though she knows there is no way I can really

understand, she will pat my hand and say, "There, there now, try and settle down."

The things the Indian people went through were bad. The things the Jewish people went through, just a generation ago, were worse.

Moving On

In 2012, Martha flew up to Columbus, Ohio. She and I agreed that I would fly up toward the end of her visit, spend a couple of days, and fly home with her. Worked for me. Two days with relatives is about my limit.

You have to understand, you can't fly anywhere from Oklahoma City unless you go through Dallas, so after a two-hour layover in Dallas I boarded flight 223 for Columbus, Ohio. I entered the plane with only my briefcase in hand and started down the aisle, passing through first class. There was a young man in front of me carrying a small duffle.

As we approached my row, the young man in front of me started jamming the small duffle into the overhead above my row with more force than necessary. I had number 13C, I always ask for an aisle seat.

Sitting in seat 13B was an old woman, very pale, thin white hair, with heavy make-up. She held on to her seat with a lethal grip. She lifted her right hand and pointed a bony finger at the young man and actually yelled, "You know my coat is up there? You're mashing my coat. You think it's nothing? I tell you what!"

She raised both her hands towards the young man. "Throw the coat down here, I'll put it on the floor and step on it, would you like that? I have a suitcase up there too, throw that down, I'll step on that too, you like that? Throw the coat down, I'll tear it before I step on it, you like that?"

The young man stood, entranced, holding his duffle, half in, half out.

The old woman yelled at him, "Well, what, what do you want," all the time gesturing at the young man with bony arms and hands, blue eyes blazing.

Everyone was watching. He slowly pulled his duffle from the overhead and with tight cheeks, proceeded down the aisle toward the back.

I was next.

I fell into seat number 13C, not looking at the ogre in 13B and placed my briefcase under the seat in front of me pushing it as far forward as possible.

In my side vision, I could feel the watcher.

I set my seatbelt, closed my eyes, and set about removing myself from the situation. I can do that. Several decades ago, I actually slept through the first Ninja Turtles movie with our children. I escaped, Martha couldn't. I paid for that.

An hour and a half from Dallas, I heard the pilot announce our approach and I sat up. The old woman, seated next to her husband, was getting herself ready. I casually asked her, "Do you all live here in Columbus?"

She looked up at me with the most precious face and said, "We lived here most of our lives. We live now in California. Why, only God knows. Our children are here now, and our grandchildren, so we come to visit. We are from Germany, this old man and me." She gestured toward the old man to her left. "We met in Germany. We were both in the camps, you know. That's› where we met.

"My parents died there. His too. We had no hope. Then the Americans came.

"The Presbyterian Church in Columbus sponsored us and brought us here to Columbus. We had nothing. We spoke no English. They saved us. We got married, this old man and me", she pointed at him with her chin.

She elbowed her husband and he jolted awake. "Wake up, you. We're having a conversation here."

He lifted an eyelid, glanced at me, pointed at the old woman with his chin, and said, "Isn't she wonderful, this woman I married?" The old woman's face softened and fell slightly. She took the old man's right arm in hers and held him close.

It was quiet for a few moments then she turned her head towards me and said, "This old man, he thinks I'm wonderful. Should I ask for more? This old man and me looked into the face of hell and came out holding hands. We've held hands for sixty-five years and we've never been more than a breath away from one another, never more than a heartbeat."

Isn't she wonderful?

Isn't she wonderful?

OY.

Cloak of Freedom was painted during the 2016 election, depicting only the freedom found in the United States.

Mike Larsen waving at the crowd for being recognized as the "Honored One."

The Pedestal

2006

After many years as an artist, having achieved awards, prizes, lots of praise, it can be easy to place yourself on a pedestal, plastic of course.

A number of years ago, I was honored in a show as the "Honored One," given special recognition, a monetary prize, and a parade! The big day came for the parade. It was full of dignitaries and a band. I was so proud.

They placed me in a new BMW convertible where I was to set on the deck and wave at the crowd. The lady who drove the BMW also owned the car and continually gave me the look for having my boots on her new back seat.

The parade started.

We had only gone a couple of blocks and I was just waving my ass off when I looked to my right. And, there in the crowd was an old man looking at me, an Indian. He was at least ninety. He was short and wore a really tall black hat. He was very dapper looking with sharply creased pants, a white western shirt with silver on the collar tips, and a large silver bolo with a turquoise stone in the middle.

We made eye contact and held it. It was as if slow motion took over time. I looked at him and he looked at me. There was no sound.

No one there but he and me.

We continued to look at one another as the crowd slowly moved around us. It seems as though I could hear the band. I looked at him and he at me.

As I looked at him his face changed and I could see that that he was going to speak. He lifted his head a little and slowly his mouth opened. He was going to speak. I watched him and even cupped my ear and looked at him and listened.

I looked at him and he looked at me and said, "Get down from there you damned fool!"

I climbed down from my pedestal.

Speaking Catholic

2011

If it were not for Mary, there would be no need for Faith.

My granddad, my Papa, was a sharecropper in the early part of the 1900's. For years he worked a piece of land south of Wynnewood, Oklahoma, owned by a man who had come from the East and bought up most of the land in the area. Grandma and Papa had six kids, four girls and two boys. They all learned pretty quick that hard work was the order of the day. Sunday was just another workday.

The only exception was when a Camp Meeting would be in the area. On those Sundays, everyone would get cleaned up, pile in the wagon, and go get saved.

Mother's first experience with an organized church was after she married at age fourteen. She and Dad, age thirty-five, moved to Oklahoma City. Dad was a Deacon in the Baptist Church. He sang in the choir and occasionally would be called to preach. He had a wandering eye.

Shortly after I was born, in 1944, he and Mother were divorced. When I was four years old, I contracted polio and Mother and I moved to Dallas so I could be in the hospital for treatment. Mother had to work. No more church for a while. She worked every Sunday. Two shifts.

After a while, I went back to live with Grandma and Papa in Wynnewood.

The Sacred Heart by Mike Larsen remains in the artist's private collection.

Mother stayed in Dallas to work.

In Wynnewood, I was introduced to the church of Christ, which is where Grandma went. Papa simply couldn't tolerate church, so he stayed home.

I figure there must have been probably fourteen or fifteen churches of Christ in Wynnewood, and just as many Baptist. There were some other churches over in colored town. Those churches didn't have names, but they had good music.

Mother bought a café in Wynnewood in 1951 or so and after a few years of courtship, married my stepfather. After another few years, we all moved to Amarillo, Texas. My stepfather was a First Christian, but he had not always been. He was born in Denmark in the late 1800's. He and his parents came to the USA and settled in Dallas.

My stepfather's mother, from the very first day, started making plans for him to study for, and finally become, a Lutheran minister. A fine plan, I'm sure.

He went to college at Southern Methodist University, then went to seminary, always assured by his mother that her plans for him were the right ones. "God would be pleased," she said.

In his second year of seminary, he and a dozen or so other young men with a plan went on a retreat north of Dallas to pray, contemplate, search their souls, smoke cigarettes, and drink two very large jars of "shine."

It was my stepdad's turn, so he went out to the well to draw water. The "shine" had to be well watered down. He went out to the well and discovered the bucket was already down. He pulled the rope and lifted the bucket up. It was heavy. He rested the bucket on the lip of the well and took a dipper full of the cool well water to sooth his burning throat. He reached in again with the dipper. Looking up at him with eyes straight out of Revelation was a large coiled copperhead, its tongue tasting the air, judging the fear in it.

My stepdad pushed the bucket back down the well and ran, stopping every few steps to vomit. When he got back to Dallas, he went immediately to his mother to tell her that he could never be what she wanted. Never. She was struck dumb and took to her bed in tears, not to be seen again for two days.

He was sorry to disappoint her so badly but he had, no doubt about it, come face to face with the Serpent, and lived. My stepdad never again went into a Lutheran Church.

Martha was born and raised Catholic but she married a Presbyterian. She relented and became Presbyterian too. She had become Presbyterian but always, in her heart, she was Catholic. Over the course of several years, she had two fine sons, but her marriage didn't work out. After a period of time she and I met at the Oklahoma City Festival of the Arts and both our lives changed.

We were married in the Presbyterian Church and continued to attend there. When we moved to Perkins, Oklahoma, our lives changed again as Martha's need to return to her roots was so very strong. She needed to return to the Catholic Church.

I told her I would go with her to Mass but not to expect me to participate, thank you very much. We started going to St. Francis Catholic Church in Stillwater, and against all my better judgments, over time, I started listening. And hearing. It seems I had questions all my adult life. Suddenly, I heard answers.

During this period, we had moved my mother, who was in failing health, to Perkins. We found her a small house not too far from us. She seemed content and I would go by every day to visit. One day after my visit, I got up to leave. She waved a crooked finger at me, cleared her throat with a rasp, and said, "Sit." I sat. She gave me a look and said, in her 93-year-old voice, "Well, have you learned to speak Catholic, yet?"

In 2011, we attended a Catholic Mass north of Dallas with our youngest son's future in-laws. It was the biggest church I had ever been in. There must have been two- or three-thousand people there. We had to sit toward the back. Martha and I had taken our seats as I watched a young woman sit in the pew in front of us. She sat in front of Martha, to the right of me. She was smooth of face, with dark hair, as far as I could tell. There was a touch of white high on her forehead mostly covered with a light blue veil, which softly fell down her back over a light blue Habit. She was a Nun.

I watched her all during the Mass as she kept a Rosary clutched to her heart. When it came time, and the Priest lifted the Cup, the Cup of Christ's Blood, her lips trembled and a tear fell from her eye and slowly traced down her cheek. Her trembling lips slowly formed a smile. This woman, who I did not speak to, who I will never see again, changed my life.

When Mary journeyed to visit her cousin, Elizabeth, the door opened and Elizabeth looked out at her cousin, a young woman, smooth of face, with dark hair, a light blue veil covering her head, and falling softly down her back.

Hail Mary, full of Grace.

Yes, Mother. I have learned to speak Catholic.

Martha Larsen posed for Mike when he was painting *The Assumption of Mary.*

An old drawing Mike Larsen discovered in one of his sketch books, most likely from the 1960's.

LEO

A few years ago, we started daily visits to an elderly couple here in town. The old man was ninety, his wife a bit older. We very seldom saw the wife, as she tended to sleep most of the day. These visits were at the behest of our church.

Our job was simple, fill the old man's nebulizer and stay for a short visit. The old man's name was Leo and he and I became good friends as time passed by. I would go into his living room and he would have the nebulizer in one hand and a Camel cigarette in the other. He was a life-long chain smoker. It was a constant complaint of his that the damned cigarettes were five bucks a pack.

Every once in a while, Leo would lean back in his old chair, take a puff of his smoke, point at me with the nebulizer, and say, "You know, I recall a story that you need to hear." I had come to understand by now that it was time for me to just take a seat and pay attention.

"Back around 1950 or 1951, I had quite a number of cows on a piece of land north and east of Lawton. Had another piece leased, but it was west of Lawton about twenty miles or so. Me and my hired man would work and feed the cows on the one piece then drive over to the west side and work those. I had a pretty good Dodge pickup at the time. My hired man was a good worker but I always wished that he bathed more. Anyways, about half way between these two pieces of land we passed by a farm owned by an old lady. Her husband had up and disappeared quite a few years back. On the west side of her farm, about a half-mile from her house, was a huge pecan tree forty or fifty yards off the road. You couldn't see the house from the tree. I love pecans and every time we passed by that place, my hired man would say, 'We should stop and take some of those pecans.' I never was big on stealing, but I was weak when I was young. And I did love pecans.

"The next morning when I picked him up, my man threw several tow sacks in the back of my Dodge and off we went. The sun wasn't up yet so we went on and fed the cows east of Lawton first. Around eleven o'clock or so, we headed west thinking we could spend our lunch hour picking pecans. We stopped along the fence line, climbed over the fence, and sacks in hand headed for that tree. Lunch hour came and went and about three o'clock we had picked four sacks full of pecans.

"I was smoking a cigarette when I first heard the truck. It was coming from the direction of the old lady's house. Too far to make a run for it so we just stood still. Here she come, in an old Ford truck, black as night. She came in headed straight at me and stopped about a foot from where I stood. She slowly got out, reached back in the cab, and pulled out the biggest double barrel shotgun I ever saw. She was a small woman and how the hell she held that thing up I'll never know, but she did and she pointed it right at my nose.

"I was looking back at two of the blackest holes I ever saw. Over those holes I was looking at two old grey eyes, but mostly I was looking at her left eye which seemed to move around on its own like one of those lizards you see on TV."

Mike Larsen and his cousin Roy.

"Boys!" she said.

"Ma'am." I said.

"What the hell are you two sons a bitches up to?"

"Well ma'am, we knew you lived alone and so we just thought we'd pick a few of these pecans for you seeing as how you might not be able, Ma'am," the whole time I kept trying to spot what her left eye was seeing.

She kept the 12 pointed at my nose and said, "that's mighty kind of you two sons a bitches so you might as well put them sacks in the back of my Ford." Which we did. "So's you'll know, I don't expect I'll be needing any more pecans."

"She pitched the 12-gauge into the cab of the Ford, crawled in, and off she went. We stood there for a few minutes. My hired man said quite a few things in Mex. I don't know what. We walked back to my Dodge and went to tend the cows. It was very late when I finally got home that night. All I could think about was losing 300 pounds of the finest paper shell pecans in Comanche County. Even if I had stole the damned things, I ain't had a pecan in over sixty years."

"Don't ever steal!"

I've said that many times when I used to teach and I always had to explain. Copying someone's style is stealing. Copying someone's painting is stealing if you intend to sell the work. We have seen many times at shows, an artist has directly copied the work of another person.

Developing a style is difficult, takes a long time, and involves very hard work. I understand all that, but it is incredibly rewarding if your style is just your own. Just your own.

I won't steal. Maybe it's because I'm afraid there might be a lingering, bitter taste in my mouth of pecans from 1951 or possibly having to look down side-by-side tunnels to hell with a wondering old grey eye just above.

Ruth Larsen and Otto "Papa" Carter.

CRUTCHES

LATE 1940'S AND 2013

Once in a while, we all need a crutch.

When I was three or four years old, I contracted polio. It was 1947, a year before a man named Jonas Salk started working on the vaccine.

My mother, bless her heart, was really pressed. We went to Dallas so I could be in the hospital for treatment. Mother worked as a waitress, double shifts.

One day an older man, who was a regular customer, asked her about her family and she told him about me. He studied her for a moment and said, "Ruth, I belong to the Elks. Let me see what I can do."

She didn't hear anything for a week or so, not expecting to, then the older gent she had talked to and half a dozen other well-dressed men came into the café where she worked. They asked her to sit, and she did. The older man said to my mother, "The Elks will pay for all the medical expenses for your son." Knowing my mother, she didn't cry, until later.

These men all came to visit me while I was in the Dallas hospital. I don't remember them. I wish I did.

I have never thought of things in life as being preordained, but I do believe that opportunity might slap us around to get our attention as it offers us something wonderful. Polio affected my right arm and leg, consequently making me a "lefty" and changing the patterns of my thinking. Though I sometimes curse the weakness of my right side, I am also thankful for the many blessings resulting from the illness I had.

In 1963, when I graduated from high school, me and four guys I ran with, without telling our parents, went down to join the Army. The four guys I ran with were all accepted. I was rejected because of the Polio. I was lucky. Two of my buds came home. Two stayed…in Viet Nam.

When I was four and in therapy, a doctor in Houston designed the cutest pair of crutches for me. They didn't look like regular crutches, but more like tools of some kind, simple with a handle and straps at the top. I kept those crutches at Mother's house until the early 1980's when my brother found them and included them in a garage sale he was having. He sold them for fifty cents. He also sold several of my paintings for two dollars each. Spilt milk. What ya' gonna do?

I used crutches several times in my young life because of surgeries. Surgeries performed by the same doctor who made my crutches in 1947.

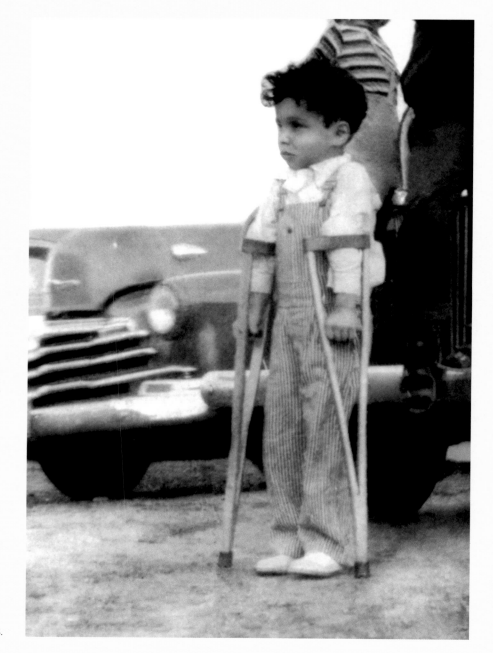

Mike Larsen in Luling, Texas, with his "special" crutches.

Overcoming the necessity of crutches over the years made me more determined to be self-sufficient and solitary, things I believe you will find in most artists. My wife is like that. Her obstacles were different, but had to be overcome. She is a great artist, very self-reliant and determined as hell.

On one of the last visits I made to my friend, Leo, after I had filled his nebulizer and got him a new pack of smokes from the kitchen, he said, "Sit down there, I want to tell you about an old woman I knew down in Lawton." I sat. During the course of the story, I kept thinking this was the same old woman that he had stolen pecans from in 1951.

"I knew this old lady, she lived by herself on a place north of Lawton. I don't know what went with her husband. These were hard times back then and there were lots of men on the road looking for handouts. I know the old woman kept a sizable garden out back of the house and I also know that she had a brand new, green, garden hoe that she highly prized. I suspect her daughter bought it for her. Her daughter lived in Lawton and worked for the phone company.

"Anyways, one day the old woman was working in her kitchen when she heard a banging on the back screen door. She always kept the screen locked. She looked over to see a strange man on the porch looking in at her. He was ragged and dirty. His smell preceded him.

"'Lady,' he said, 'wonder if I could get something to eat? I ain't ate in about two days.' She was used to this, someone came to her door two, three times a week. There must have been a flag out front saying, 'Eat here.'

"'You set there on the porch, I'll bring you some food,' she said. 'Ma'am, you figure I might set at the table, I ain't set at a proper table in a while?'

"'I guess.' she said. He came in.

"She fixed him some food and even fixed fresh coffee, then went about washing the dishes. She noticed her brand new hoe leaning against the door jam and felt proud.

"The pain was like nothing the old woman had ever experienced. She fell against the sink as the roadman started hitting her on the back of her head. He beat her black and blue, up one side and down the other, finally knocking her to the floor breaking her hip. He yelled at her, demanding money, but she couldn't hear him. The pain was screaming.

"The roadman stole everything he could find, kicked her in the side, and ran out the door. He considered the new hoe but passed it by.

"She lay on the floor. It was quiet.

"The phone rang. Quiet again.

"The phone rang.

"Quiet.

"Her daughter at the phone company couldn't understand why her momma was not answering and began to worry. She called several times during the course of the afternoon and at exactly five o'clock jumped in her Ford on her way to the old woman.

"She drove into the side yard and let out a breath. There was her mother, in the garden. She was standing in the garden among the rows of tomatoes and peas.

"The old woman had pulled herself up using one of the dining chairs and somehow located a length of two by four and fashioned herself a crutch. She had nailed her belt to one end to use as a strap that would fit over her shoulder. She was standing in the garden with that handmade crutch jammed up under her armpit with a strap over her shoulder holding it half way down with one hand. In her other hand she was holding a brand new hoe, chopping weeds."

A crutch can be a fine, innovative tool, or a fiercely demanding master.

We have known artists over the years that have used crutches of one kind or another, for one reason or another. Some actually use it as a shield against success. One artist friend of ours uses crutches to hold himself up while he paints. He is a quadriplegic, the most prolific artist I know. I'm sure, when he was young, he cursed his body and screamed

at circumstance. He could have spent his life in a motorized chair, with people to wait on him. He chose not to.

Seems, there is always a choice.

Except for one thing.

Leo died a few days ago.

I wasn't there, but went over after. I got there about the same time as the Priest. The house smelled the same and as usual, was all a clutter. Leo was on the floor, on his back, straight as a board. He had on a cowboy shirt, stiffly ironed, and jeans that were too big and a huge belt buckle that he always wore. His hair was a mess and he hadn't shaved in a few days. He had always threatened to forget the whole damned thing and grow a beard.

A nearly full pack of Lucky Strikes was trying to escape from his shirt pocket. Leo was dead, but he died with his boots on. They were new boots with high tops, red with the design of longhorn cattle running.

Ruth Larsen and Mike on a visitation day at the hospital in Luling, Texas.

One of the many rainbows Mike and Martha Larsen have chased.

THE RAINBOW

1999

Martha and I had taken several paintings to a collector over in Wewoka and were on our way back to Oklahoma City. It had been raining all day, but lucky for us the storms had moved to our east and the skies were clear and bright for our return trip. It was probably raining like hell in Tulsa about then.

We had taken Highway 56 north out of Wewoka, which would take us up to the interstate. We had gone only a couple of miles when out the passenger side windows, almost suddenly, there appeared a rainbow against those dark skies to our east.

I pulled off the two-lane onto the grass to look because the end of the rainbow hit the ground no more than forty or fifty yards from our car. Martha and I both got out to look. Of course, I didn't have my camera. We walked over to the fence line and just stood there, looking. I've seen many rainbows, but none like this. Forty yards away, maybe fifty. "I'll be right back," I said and climbed the fence. I walked into the field toward the rainbow.

I wander.

I kept walking and walking. It didn't seem like it was raining but I was suddenly soaking wet, and I wasn't any closer to the rainbow than when I started. How strange. I looked back at Martha and she was waving and saying something, but I couldn't hear her. I turned back and kept walking toward the rainbow. After a while it became clear that, for whatever reason, I wasn't going to get close so I stopped.

I turned back toward the car and saw Martha in the distance. She had her hands to her mouth. I walked back. I kept looking over my shoulder and, as I knew it would be, the rainbow was still there. I reached the fence line and looked back. Still there. Forty to fifty yards away.

I climbed the fence and stood there with Martha. She held my arm and we looked at it. Directly, she looked over at me and said, "Where were you?"

"What do you mean?"

"You went into the color. I couldn't see you. Where were you?"

"But Martha, I never got to the color."

We stood there for a while, looking until there was nothing there but distant storms. We went back to the car and Martha found an old dry shirt for me to put on and we drove home.

It seems like Martha and I have always been chasing rainbows. Always have. Always will.

I don't understand the phenomenon that happened that day, but I accept it without question.

Rainbows are perfect. I am not. Perfection is not in my grasp. I can't remember a painting that I have done that even approached perfection and I'm completely happy with that. Maybe, one of these days, I'll gain a dab of understanding about art and I'm happy about that too.

Perhaps the idea of being an artist is like looking for something you know you can't have. The joy is in the doing. Twenty or so years ago I began putting a small rainbow under my signature. I don't believe I knew why until now, as I write this story.

I will live out my life as an artist, seeking something illusive and hopefully improving along the way, knowing that truly, the adventure is the art.

Ebony by Mike Larsen.

Mike Larsen and longtime friend and collector Darryl Smette.

WALKING THE DOG

2013

Montana is beautiful. The area around Red Lodge is probably one of the most beautiful in the country. Right on up there with Perkins, Oklahoma.

Two or three years ago, Martha and I went to Red Lodge with friends who owned a fine home half way up one of the mountains south of town. We were there for a solid week, had a very relaxed time, and ate lots of really good food. The place where we ate breakfast each morning had come highly rated and I quickly found out why. They served sausage gravy on everything. Burp.

Being off in the mountains for an extended time, one tends to notice all the small things in order to keep from going bonkers because there is little to do except climb the mountain, a thing I am loath to do.

Reno's Crossing by Mike Larsen.

Sitting on the balcony one afternoon, Scotch in hand, we noticed a bright red suburban going very slow along the road in front of the house. Guesses were passed around as we tried to figure out just why the hell he was going so slow. Car trouble? Drunk? Sightseeing? Perplexing, for sure. As the huge car got closer, our question was answered. A small white dog that looked like a Rat Terrier with a beard was walking alongside the car. It had on a leash that disappeared into the open driver's window. The man in the car was simply taking his dog for a walk.

I'm sure the little white animal believed, happily, that his master, in his kindness, was taking him for a nice afternoon stroll. But of course, as everyone knows, dogs will believe anything.

Wild Ones by Mike Larsen.

BRAVERY

A day trip had been planned, so off we went, north then east to visit the Custer Battlefield. When we got there, Martha and I bypassed the Tourist Center where a man in a brown uniform was holding a captive audience in his hands with a well-practiced narrative. We walked up the hill and stood just above where Custer and most of the Seventh Cavalry were killed. We stood for a long time. A hot wind trying to push us away.

We looked down a winding ravine that led down to the Greasy Grass River and the Indian encampment just beyond. There were markers scattered here and there all the way down to the river, markers where young men had fallen trying to escape blistering fire, young men rushing to this high place to make breastworks with their horses. Time ran out. Ammunition ran out too, except for that last saved bullet.

I cannot imagine the bravery, or the fear. Both have a smell, and the smell was heavy on the air. They all died. They all died that day, men and animals. Be still and listen, you can hear the horses screaming. The horses didn't understand. They didn't understand, because they couldn't. I was glad when we left that place.

I have no doubt that Custer was a very brave man. We have known many brave men, but bravery like his is like an exceptionally fine sword, it must be well tempered.

Stone Pony by Mike Larsen.

The stamp created by Mike Larsen in celebration of Oklahoma's Centennial.

WHAT A STATE

Sometimes the winds don't blow, the rivers don't flow, and the sky ain't blue.

In the late 1830's, the Chickasaw people left their homelands in the East and came, reluctantly, to Oklahoma. They were allowed the western portion of Choctaw land. The Choctaw had already, reluctantly, been sent here. The people were promised this land, in common, for as long as rivers flow, grass grows, and the sky is blue.

This is Oklahoma though, and as they say, "If you don't like the weather, wait ten minutes, it'll change." Seems like politics is a little like that. Politicians swarmed into Oklahoma as the new state erupted with growing pains, and lots of Indian land, lots of Indian land.

A new government was rapidly coming to our state and the capital was going to be Guthrie. The fellow who came up with the name, Guthrie, no doubt had a bad cold at the time. Guth...rie. Bless you.

The capital newspapers were run at the time by, oh no, Republicans. "We can't have that" said a daring Governor Charles Haskell. In a midnight raid, in 1910, he sent a number of, no doubt well-armed, fellows to Guthrie to seize the State Seal and whisk it to Oklahoma City. A new state capital was born.

Oklahoma City was now the capital of Oklahoma, headquartered in the Huckins Hotel. Guthrie ain't got over it in a hundred years, which leads us to...

The Conductor in front of the Civic Center Music Hall in Oklahoma City.

THE OKLAHOMA CENTENNIAL

We had quite a run of good fortune leading up to the Centennial of Oklahoma in 2007. We were commissioned to do a couple of monumental bronzes that now live at the Civic Center Music Hall in Oklahoma City. One is a symphony conductor, the other is a ballerina on point. Both bronzes are nine feet tall. Both bronzes were produced at a foundry in Lubbock, Texas. The only thing I can say about Lubbock is, I enjoyed looking at it in my rear view mirror.

Mike Larsen and Yvonne Chouteau in front of the sculpture of the prima ballerina in the lobby of the Civic Center Music Hall in downtown Oklahoma City.

Mike Larsen at the foundry in Lubbock inspecting the sculpture for the Civic Center Music Hall of Yvonne Chouteau.

WITH THESE HANDS

CHICKASAW ARTIST MIKE LARSEN PAINTS A PICTURE OF OKLAHOMA THROUGH SOULFUL PORTRAITS
AND INSPIRING LANDSCAPES, A BODY OF WORK BEFITTING THE 2006 OKLAHOMAN OF THE YEAR.

mike [LARSEN]

OKLAHOMAN OF THE YEAR

By Brooke Adcox

ACCORDING TO LEGEND, Native Americans refused to be photographed out of a belief that the image could steal their souls. Chickasaw artist Mike Larsen, then, is in the business of painting souls. Using canvas and oil paint rather than celluloid and flashbulbs, Larsen has spent the majority of his life capturing the essence of his subjects one brush stroke at a time.

His works feature thoughtful eyes; strong facial features; compelling body positions; dramatic backgrounds; brilliant colors; and expressive, oversized hands—all of which combine to make each painting and sculpture come alive to tell its story. Through subjects like Oklahoma's Native American ballerinas, Indian shamans, the legendary Pistol Pete, and the elders of his own Chickasaw tribe, Larsen paints a picture of Oklahoma that is respectful, historically accurate, expressive, imaginative, powerful, and most important, honorable.

"Mike Larsen has an amazing ability to understand and bring to the canvas the true personality and character of the people he paints," says Chickasaw Governor Bill Anoatubby. "Each of his paintings tells a unique story. He establishes a respectful relationship with his subject that is expressed in his final work."

Often discussed in the company of famous Oklahoma Native American artists Woody Crumbo, Acee Blue Eagle, and Jerome Tiger, this soft-spoken, humble man would sooner talk about his gratitude to be a working artist than the magnitude and effect his work has on the Native American and Oklahoma art communities.

"We are losing a lot of our master artists," says Betty Price, executive director of the Oklahoma Arts Council. "Mike is a bridge into this century in terms of Native American artists who

Mike Larsen in his Perkins studio with his most recently completed painting, *Sings to God*

are here and have made such great contributions to our state."

In 2006, Larsen had a record year of giving back to his home state. He was recognized as the Red Earth Honored One in June, saw one of his paintings selected to adorn the Centennial stamp in September, completed twenty-four portraits of Chickasaw elders the same month, and worked on two larger-than-life Centennial sculptures for the Oklahoma City Civic Center through October. "It seems like all of a sudden, but not all of a sudden, we are astoundingly busy," he says.

But 2006 isn't Larsen's first big splash onto the art scene; this sixty-two-year-old has steadily been developing his craft as a professional artist in Oklahoma for more than thirty-five years. A self-described working-class Oklahoman—who wears blue jeans, collared shirts, and broken-in cowboy boots—Larsen drives a GMC Yukon to and from his downtown Perkins studio six days a week and often tells his best friend and fellow artist Harvey Pratt that he is "Paintin' pictures. That's what I do, paint pictures."

Modesty aside, Larsen thoroughly researches the smallest details of every painting or sculpture. With so many of his subjects historical and Native American figures, he spends an exhaustive amount of time with his nose in books. But even more important, Larsen continually seeks to express what he values as the most important element of art, emotion.

"I paint people in an action before or after an event: That's where the emotion is," says Larsen. "If you are playing a game, you are totally involved in it. But afterward, you are tired if you lost or elated that you won. It's the emotion before or after the event I try to capture."

JANUARY/FEBRUARY 2007 **OKLAHOMA TODAY** 23

Oklahoma Today chose us for "Oklahoman of the Year." That was a big deal when you consider that I didn't play basketball, toot the flute, or "sang" country. But the most exciting thing came in a very small package. I was chosen to produce the 2007 Oklahoma Centennial Stamp.

As I have said before, I am a people painter. People always come first. There might be a landscape or skyscape in the background, but always as a secondary element. Then a funny thing happened. We moved to Perkins.

In the country, you can watch the sun rise. More than that, you can watch what is happening to the sky before the sun rises. Our home faces the east. Every morning Martha and I would sit on the front porch, coffee in hand, and watch.

Too glorious.

Mike Larsen was featured in *Oklahoma Today* Magazine as part of Oklahoma's many centennial celebrations.

I started painting these skyscapes and some mornings we would go to the bridge that crosses the Cimarron south of town and shoot dozens of photos that would later become paintings.

Martha came up to the studio one day and several of the sunrise paintings were leaning against the wall. "I think we need to put these on our web site," she said. And she did, that very day, the very day that the director and the entire board of the United States Postal Service sat around their inlaid table and, for whatever reason, pulled up our web site for a peek.

They were looking for something different for the Oklahoma Centennial Stamp. No horses, no cows or cowboys, no oil wells, no country singers. Pure Oklahoma beauty was what they were after.

Timing is everything.

Ain't it the truth.

The images the United States Postal Service viewed on the Larsens' website that prompted their interest in Mike Larsen as the artist to create the Centennial Stamp for Oklahoma.

Yvonne Chouteau and Mike Larsen at the dedication of *Flight of Spirit*.

Yvonne

St. Joseph's Cathedral in downtown Oklahoma City is a magnificent church. It was beautiful in its beginning and has remained so in its age. We were there for the funeral of our friend Yvonne Chouteau Terekhov. Yvonne died January 24, 2016. St. Joe's was the perfect place to say goodbye to her. Like the church, Yvonne was incredible when she was young and was beautiful on the very day she died at the age of 86.

Martha and I first met Yvonne in 1991 as we began preparations to paint the mural, *Flight of Spirit* for the State Capitol. Yvonne lived in Oklahoma City so it was convenient to visit her home in Crown Heights. We always called first before going to her home and we never had to knock, she would have been watching for us. The door would open and there would be that face... that smile. One hand on the door, the other on her hip, she would wave the air aside and usher us in. The dogs would be there, of course, golden and soft. Should we let a hand fall to our side, there would be a fine golden head there, ready for a scratch, ears ready for a ruffle, a big wet tongue our reward.

I remember never feeling like I was in the presence of someone so important, a legend, an icon. Martha and I were simply in the home of a friend, a friend who just happened to have astounding photos of two vibrant young ballet dancers casually sitting around. As we would look around the room, there would be photographs of the others, Maria and Marjorie, Moscelyne and Roman, and Rosella. Martha and I drink in history like a really good wine so we always felt pleasantly full when we left Yvonne's house, the dogs escorting us to our car. I always wanted to stay longer, maybe spend the day, not doing anything, just being with her.

For the mural project we rented a warehouse for six months. The building was large enough to house the mural, which was 22 feet long and 11 feet tall. When Yvonne would come to the warehouse studio, she would always bring a giant bag of Fritos. She would wander back to the painting, stand some distance away from it at what I call "Ballet Rest," and study the work for some time. We would both be quiet. After a bit, she would move closer to the painting and move her open hands along, almost but not quite, touching the canvas. Then she would back away. We would sit. Eat Fritos. And visit.

In the early development of the mural, when I was creating drawings or idea sketches, she would offer

Kate, Mike Larsen's daughter, presented flowers to Yvonne Chouteau at the dedication of *Flight of Spirit*.

advice, but only if I asked for it. She was not one to volunteer an opinion. She seemed to really enjoy watching the painting grow. She continued to visit me at my Paseo Studio through the years, Frito's in hand.

With the mural finished and hung at the Capitol, a dedication was held. All five of the ballerinas represented in the painting were there, for the first time. All together, at one time.

They had five tiny ballerinas present roses to each of these great women. Our daughter, Kate, age five, presented a bouquet of red roses to Yvonne. Yvonne thanked Kate with that smile. Kate was with us at Yvonne's funeral.

Several years ago, Yvonne became ill. It became clear, only among her family, Miguel, Elizabeth, and Christina, that she was developing Alzheimer's, that thief of mind and beauty. Miguel cared for her as best he could and as long as he could. Then Miguel...Miguel Terekhov, died. Yvonne's daughters took over the care of their mother, Elizabeth with her every day, for years. Yvonne died at her home, surrounded by her family...and her dogs.

Martha and I will always carry her memory with us, not the memory of a lovely prima ballerina, but the memory of one of the best friends we ever had. Thank you, Yvonne, for what you gave us. Thank you God, for what you gave Yvonne.

God touched Yvonne when she was four years old. She touched us all for the rest of her long life.

Yvonne Chouteau...Yvonne "Toe-Shoe." Martha and I will miss you.

Yvonne Chouteau and Miguel Terekhov at the University of Oklahoma.

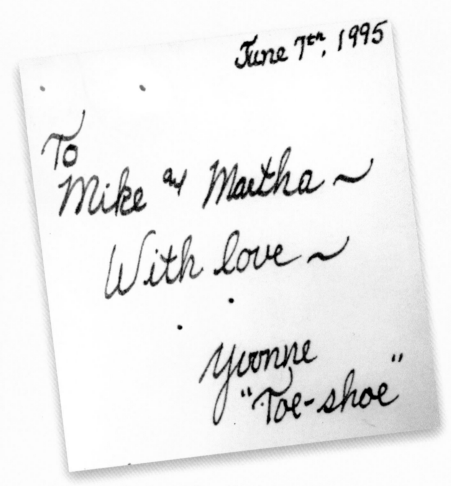

A note from Yvonne Chouteau to Mike and Martha Larsen.

Mike and Martha Larsen following the 2015 Oklahoma Hall of Fame Banquet & Induction Ceremony.

THE 2015 OKLAHOMA HALL OF FAME . . .
TWO NIGHTS BEFORE ZERO HOUR

2015

The auditorium was crowded with students; they looked to be of junior high age. The stage was small, like the stages of most schools. Even though I was to be one of the speakers, it was left up to me to get the set-up on the stage ready. There were going to be four of us speaking, Martha, my niece, me, and someone I didn't know.

I took up a folding card table and four chairs. The card table looked familiar. Next, I took up two glasses of water, one for me and one for Martha. At the table she would be sitting at my left.

The crowd grew anxious and there was much chatter amongst the students.

After the four of us seated ourselves at the table, a man entered the stage from the right. He was dressed completely in leather from head to toe. His hair was long and greasy. He was carrying his own chair. He placed it between me and Martha and sat. He spread his legs out in such a fashion that both Martha and I had to scoot our chairs back.

He took a drink of water from Martha's glass. He was Martha's ex-husband.

My niece stepped up to the microphone and announced me as the first speaker.

I stood. I suddenly realized that my speech was written out on my t-shirt, which was under my chambray shirt, which was under my sweater. I tried to get to my t-shirt, but for some reason I couldn't get my sweater off.

I excused myself and left the stage to find a restroom. I walked down a long hall that had no lights. I had to feel my way along the wall until I finally found it. Inside the restroom I took off my sweater and chambray shirt. I stared into the mirror at my t-shirt that had my speech written on it. My speech was completely smeared and unreadable.

I walked out of the restroom wondering what I was going to do. Standing right outside the door was a supreme court justice, in full black robe and high heels, pointing a long finger at me. She said, "It is my judgment that you left your speech at home." Having said that, she turned and walked away down the dark hall, high heels clicking.

"Good God," I thought, home is an hour away.

I ran out of the building into the parking lot to get my car. Two hours at least, there and back. I ran into the parking lot. There were thousands of cars there. Thousands. They all looked like mine.

My eyes opened. It was 5:30 a.m.

The Oklahoma Hall of Fame Class of 2015, from left, Jim Halsey, William J. Ross, Sharen Jester Turney, Steadman Upham, Kevin Durant, Bill Hancock, and Mike Larsen.

The 2015 Oklahoma Hall of Fame . . .
One Night Before Zero Hour

As I stood before an amazing dinner crowd of thousands, and having been introduced and idolized properly, I stood at the podium awash, awash in bright light. The band had just finished up a rousing rendition of "Oh What a Beautiful Morning."

I stood and delivered a magnificent speech. Women were openly weeping at its passion. I finished to cheers of adoration as flowers floated onto the stage around me. I backed away from the podium, the Oklahoma Hall of Fame award hanging around my neck heavy with its gold and diamonds.

There was a moment of absolute silence. I was suddenly staring into thousands of eyes filled with shock, then faces full of teeth as shock turned into howls of laughter and people were pointing...at me.

I suddenly felt cold.

I looked down. Dropping down from my tuxedo coat and white shirt were two very white, very thin saplings with argyle socks at their roots falling into a puddle of expensive black cloth with shiny strips appearing here and there, well-polished black shoe tips peeking out.

I opened my eyes. It was 5:30 a.m.

Ken Fergeson, left, presented Mike Larsen for induction into the Oklahoma Hall of Fame.

THE 2015 OKLAHOMA HALL OF FAME...
BANQUET & INDUCTION CEREMONY

I stood at the podium and looked out onto an amazing dinner crowd...

Just as a side note...I pinned my trousers to my shirt, wore a belt, extra tight, and wore suspenders that would have pleased a mule skinner.

And I remembered to take my speech.

Mike Larsen, looking at his wife Martha, while giving his acceptance remarks following receiving Oklahoma's highest honor with induction into the Oklahoma Hall of Fame.

GENERAL ADVICE

1. Don't give up your day job. I left college in the middle of my senior year because my counselor informed me I had eighteen hours of academics ahead of me to graduate. Math, history, advanced French, math, zoology, math, math, math... At the time, I had a part-time job as a short order cook and I kept it.

I had been toying with the idea of trying street shows and festivals. So, I submitted applications to several shows and in the months ahead was able to shift my time to actually selling artwork. I kept cooking part time for about another year. There is an old axiom, if you have a job, don't leave it till you have another in hand.

I soon found I could make more at art shows than I thought. Even though it was risky, I began painting full time. I have never looked back.

2. Listen to God. Listen to dogs. Listen to the wind. Listen to yourself. Don't listen to other artists.

In my second year of college, one of my counselors, an exceptional watercolorist in his own right, called me into his office and told me to sit down. "Mister Larsen" he said. I knew I was in trouble. He sat back and looked at me and said, "You need to think of a different major because as an artist you're just no damned good." As I recall, I had way too much to drink that night.

Dreams of My Father by Mike Larsen.

Mike Larsen with elements of a heroic-sized bronze installed at St. Joseph's Regional Hospital in Patterson, New Jersey.

Mike Larsen in studio working on *The Conductor*.

3. Use a little common sense. As we have all probably discovered, common sense is not so common. Most artists when they are young tend to overcomplicate the act of painting. When two or three brushes will do, they will use ten. They will put way too many colors out, using only a few. They will make many sketches to the point of creating confusion.

4. Never drink during the workday. There have been artists in history, like Winslow Homer, who were able to drink all day long and produce the most beautiful works. I don't see how they could do that and maintain clarity.

5. Your own opinion is the most important.

6. Don't ask for criticism or you will surely get it.

7. Cursing provides comfort sometimes found not even in prayer.

8. When you finish for the day, allow time to sit and visit with the day's work. Clear your mind and try not to think too much, it just gets in the way.

DRAWING

Sketching is one of the most important tools in art. I have always sketched, even when I was little. When I started in college we had a very good instructor. In fact, probably the best of the many instructors I had.

She was a hippie and wore the same sweater every day for months. No one got close enough to her to see if she smelled as bad as she looked. Anyway, she was a terrific teacher of drawing and made us work really fast. She taught us techniques that I use to this day.

She could draw a figure starting with the head and flowing through the form to the end of an outstretched finger or a graceful foot to the toe with one line, her tool never leaving the paper. This is called contour drawing.

I'm pretty good at it, but not as good as she was. I still incorporate the method. But, as it should be, I have modified it to suit my needs.

For an entire semester she did not allow us to use color. We could draw with anything we liked as long as it was black. Another thing she did tell us was, "If you can't draw, don't try."

I did discover years ago that my drawings need to go only so far. The sketches I do provide me with only the information necessary to begin a painting or sculpture. It is personal with me, but if I put too much enthusiasm into a drawing, the painting will sometimes suffer.

Doing a drawing for it's own sake is different. It is a pleasure, very exciting, and very much like going back to school.

Martha and I have known many artists over the years that couldn't draw their way out of a paper sack, but somehow managed to make a career for themselves in art.

Being able to draw is great, but not completely necessary. One may be really good with color or design. Some of the artists of the early 1900's were lucky cubism came into fashion, hiding many a questionable talent.

Mike Larsen teaching during the 1970's.

CHOOSING SUBJECTS

I consider myself a people painter so I'm constantly on the lookout for people that look interesting. I don't *search* for them, as I have learned that opportunity, awareness, and observation dictate.

One of my best models is a young, full-blood Chickasaw man. I have used him, probably to excess, over the years. I have been fascinated watching him grow older, always more impressive.

He has an ancient look that I have always felt that if I came across him in the forest and he was in traditional garb, I wouldn't expect him to speak English and I would approach him with my left hand on the butt of my pistol.

I have used him in many paintings and a monumental sculpture.

I tend to gravitate toward older people in general, probably because of the history that lines their faces and hands.

Sometimes subjects are chosen because of customer requirements. This is a business after all.

Mike Larsen at the AICA Show in San Demas, California, in 1995.

INSPIRATION

"Inspiration comes when the chores are done." I don't know who might have first said that, and I generally hate quotes and smarty sayings, but this one I have carried with me all my artist days.

A long time ago in my early college career, several of us "artists" were sitting around outside the art department smoking and being profound when one of the instructors walked by. She asked what we were doing and someone smirked, "waiting for inspiration to strike us." She just

turned around and walked away shaking her head. She looked back and said, "Are your chores done?" No one spoke, but I think everyone got it.

I keep a white board up on one wall of my studio where ideas, photos, words, etc. are written or taped on. It is a continual process. One of my instructors in the one semester that I studied advertising kept what he called a "morgue file." It was a very large file cabinet where he kept photos and magazine pictures filed by subject. He had been doing this for years and found it very beneficial.

I find the whole idea tedious and prefer not to be so organized. I have ideas and drawings from over the years taped up in my bathroom because for short periods of time they have a captive audience. Many, many times these drawings or idea sketches have become paintings.

Don't get me wrong, inspiration does happen once in a while. But, it is more likely to happen if you are well prepared. Are your senses toned? Are your materials ready? Is your attitude in good order? Are you constantly sketching? Are you rested? Make your own list of things that could be categorized as "chores" and I think you might be surprised at what you come up with.

Mike Larsen working on *Flight of Spirit* in the warehouse he leased to accommodate the large piece.

TIME ALONE

I would consider myself a solitary person, always have been. The only person I would welcome at any time would be my wife, Martha. In the studio working I have to be alone. Martha and I tried working together, but it just didn't work out. I tend to be very critical of my work and sometimes can turn the air blue with expletives.

Sand Hill by Mike Larsen.

A Final Word

Martha and I have three children, two boys and a girl. When she was five or six, our daughter Kate would go with me to the studio. The studio, at the time, was The Jesus is Lord Studio that burned.

Anyway, we had a little play area fixed up for her in the corner. It was complete with a cute little kitchen set that had a sink, stove, and all the tools. She seemed to really like it and didn't require much of my time.

Every once in a while though, I would be painting away and turn around to spot her leaning against the wall watching me work.

This was a precious scene that she and I often played.

She always said the same thing. "Daddy, that sure is a pretty picture."

As long as I live, that's all I want to hear from a critic.

Mike Larsen and his daughter Kate.

The Jaguar by Mike Larsen.